Contributions to Management Science

For further volumes:
http://www.springer.com/series/1505

Chiara Leardini • Gina Rossi • Sara Moggi

Board Governance in Bank Foundations

The Italian Experience

Springer

Chiara Leardini
Sara Moggi
University of Verona
Verona
Italy

Gina Rossi
University of Udine
Udine
Italy

ISSN 1431-1941 ISSN 2197-716X (electronic)
ISBN 978-3-642-41305-6 ISBN 978-3-642-41306-3 (eBook)
DOI 10.1007/978-3-642-41306-3
Springer Heidelberg New York Dordrecht London

Library of Congress Control Number: 2013958238

Printed on acid-free paper

Physica is a brand of Springer
Springer is part of Springer Science+Business Media (www.springer.com)

Foreword

The beginning of the new millennium has witnessed a dramatic surge in awareness of both the international research community and the public opinion about the crucial role played by governance structures in influencing the welfare impact of a variety of institutions, such as national states, local governments, public institutions, industrial and financial corporations, and—last but not least—nonprofit organizations (NPOs).

This general awareness of the prominent role of governance has been sadly boosted by a number of scandals that have plagued the US and Europe in the last decades. In the corporate arena, the long list of gigantic fraudulent failures includes prominent companies, such as Enron (2001), Worldcom (2002), Adelphia (2002), Tyco International (2002), Parmalat (2003), and, more recently, Bernard Madoff's Investment Fund (2008). All of those corporate scandals had an abysmal impact on the trust granted by investors, regulators, and the society at large to modern corporations and their business and accounting practices. Similarly, the financial crisis of 2007–2008 has contributed to uncover a number of sub-optimal governance structures and practices of mortgage originators (mortgage banks and brokers), hedge funds, investment banks, and credit rating agencies—arguably, the list of institutions could be much longer. The general worry about systematic governance problems in different kind of institutions has motivated researchers to describe, investigate, and sometimes challenge status-quo governance structures. This new strand of research has produced an enormous and very valuable amount of results in the intersection of law, economics, and finance.

Contributing to this fundamental and growing research area, my colleagues, Chiara Leardini, Gina Rossi, and Sara Moggi, focus in their book on the governance of Italian bank foundations, an important and fascinating type of NPOs dedicated to asset management for the purpose of grant-making. In view of both their peculiar governance characteristics and their social and economic relevance, Italian bank foundations are definitely institutions worthwhile being studied. For example, the authors show that, in spite of their nonprofit status, several Italian bank foundations manage—for the purpose of grant-making—net assets well in excess of one billion Euros.

Besides providing an extensive description of the legal origin and general characteristics of Italian bank foundations, the book offers an in-depth treatment of foundations' main organs with their respective roles and responsibilities. In particular, the book presents and discusses an impressive number of empirical facts about the composition of the Board of Trustees, the Board of Directors, as well as the local stakeholders that actually choose the Board of Trustees. Finally, an entire chapter of the book is dedicated to explaining the importance of strategic planning as a governance device for achieving the goals of NPOs in general and bank foundations in particular.

The rich set of statistics presented in the book is very informative and all major tables offer a brake-down of results by both geographic area and size. Besides showing and commenting key aggregate statistics in the two main areas of bank foundations' activities—asset management and grant-making—the authors present and discuss mini-cases and examples that guide the reader through an intriguing but complex set of topics around the governance of such institutions. In this respect, the book provides a very valuable and rigorous fact-based treatment of governance issues in Italian bank foundations that will likely attract the attention of an international readership of academics, practitioners, and interested laymen. In fact, I expect this book to have a substantial impact on the related literature and to enable further studies on the specific causal links between governance structures and economic welfare generated by Italian bank foundations.

Given the limited research attention dedicated so far to bank foundations, this book effectively fills an important research gap. It significantly contributes to the description and understanding of key elements in the governance of this specific type of nonprofit institutions. However, to take full advantage of the authors' work, I encourage the attentive reader to think even beyond the rich set of legal and statutory rules, data, facts, and anecdotes presented in the book. For example, a comparison of governance structures of Italian bank foundations with analogous structures set in place by legislators in other countries may prove useful in developing new ideas about the causal relation between the governance of NPOs and their socio-economic output.

Konstanz, November 2013 Prof., Dr. Axel Kind
Chair of Corporate Finance
University of Konstanz

Contents

Chapter 1
Italian Bank Foundations and Governance

1.1 Introduction

In the broader field of Italian nonprofit organizations, bank foundations have assumed significance in terms of the sizes of both their assets (€42,183 million as of December 31, 2012) and their grants (€965.8 million as of the same date) (ACRI 2013). Their nature as nonprofit organizations derives from the law. Under the law, bank foundations have been charged with the exclusive purpose of promoting social and economic development in a territory, beyond a profit-making intent.

Their emergence implies the need to better understand the identity of these organizations that implement a principle of horizontal subsidiarity, cooperating with public and private entities especially in the fields of art, culture, health, and social assistance. The study of Italian bank foundations can contribute to the resolution of some of the main challenges facing nonprofit organizations.

Bank foundations belong to the broader typology of foundations, defined as nonprofit groups with their own income and governing boards that use their financial resources for public benefit (European Foundation Centre 2003, 2005).

Within the nonprofit sector, foundations have some functions that are typical of nonprofit organizations, such as a serving as a substitute for the state's functions and redistributing primarily economic resources. Along with these more traditional aspects, the unique presence of income that is self-supported by assets, a system of self-governance, and donor control allows foundations to play a key role in promoting innovation and social development (Andrews 1956; Anheier 2005).

Although foundations are important to the nonprofit sector, few studies specifically consider their governance (De Andrés-Alonso et al. 2009). So that foundations do not remain "black boxes" (Diaz 1996), a thorough examination of their governance mechanisms is necessary. Some authors (Drucker 1990; Anheier 2005) have highlighted the notion that foundations, like any other nonprofit organization, have a greater need for good governance than do for-profit organizations.

The presence of different components (Handy 1990), practices, objectives, motivations, and preferences that must be brought together through the governance

C. Leardini et al., *Board Governance in Bank Foundations*, Contributions to Management Science, DOI 10.1007/978-3-642-41306-3_1,

structure reveals a growing complexity—which Anheier (2005, p. 229) defines as the "law of nonprofit complexity"—in governing and managing foundations.

The aim of the current work is to address this lack of research. Focusing in particular on Italian bank foundations, this book describes a model of governance that is coherent with the presence of relevant assets that must be used for public purposes.

This analysis of Italian bank foundations' governance uses a normative approach. In accordance with this approach, the board is identified as the body in charge with the formal authority to make decisions about mission and strategy. Consistent with rational strategic planning principles, the board states the foundation's strategy, while management implements it through actions. The study of Italian bank foundations provides a perspective on governance that can help overcome the rigidity that characterizes the typical governance model of nonprofit organizations, providing the presence of a body that acts as a link between strategic and executive functions.

The good governance of bank foundations implies that it is coherent with the specific characteristics of this type of nonprofit organization—that is, asset based and with a public purpose. A proper governance structure does not ensure per se that a foundation's mission and strategies are pursued (Hudson 1999). To that end, it is necessary to monitor, using an analytic approach, the way a board actually decides, manages, and controls the organization's activity (Middleton 1987; Ostrower and Stone 2006).

1.2 A Particular Kind of Nonprofit Organization

Foundations are a specific kind of nonprofit organization. According to the structural–operational definition provided by Salamon and Anheier (1992), an organization is defined as a nonprofit institution when it has five characteristics:

- *Organized*: It is institutionalized to some extent.
- *Private*: It is institutionally separate from government.
- *Self-governing*: It is equipped to control its own activities.
- *Not profit distributing*: It does not return profit to owners or directors.
- *Voluntary*: It involves some meaningful degree of voluntary participation.

Foundations possess such characteristics, but at the same time, they have some unique features that differentiate them from other nonprofit organizations. As Anheier (2005) notes, they are asset-based entities, created and managed for a public purpose.

Foundations derive from the transfer of assets belonging to a person or an organization to an independent entity (the foundation). The result is a nonprofit organization that manages such assets and uses the income derived from asset management for social purposes.

The choice to create a new organization, rather than give assets to a nonprofit organization already in existence, can be motivated by various reasons. As the following list shows, within prior literature, it is typical to distinguish among value-based motivations, instrumental motivations, peer pressure, and selfish motives (Anheier 2005, p. 320).

Value-based motivations

- Concern for the welfare of others, social responsibility
- Religious heritage
- Desire to repay society
- Political beliefs
- Concern with particular activities or issues
- Commitment to a specific geographical community

Instrumental motivations

- Flexibility of foundation compared with other charitable options
- Tax incentives
- Establishing a vehicle for the systematic conduct of philanthropic giving
- Memorial/dynastic motives
- Family tradition of charitable activities
- Desire to create a memorial to self
- Desire to create a family institution
- Lack of heirs

Peer pressure

- Social pressures from peers
- Fashion

Selfish motives

- Maintaining some form of control over assets
- Personal satisfaction of creating a foundation

Italian bank foundations share in their substance the common idea of foundations. They represent identifiable assets donated to a particular purpose, usually philanthropic and public in nature (Anheier 2001). Many features of bank foundations align with those that distinguish foundations in general (Anheier 2001).

Bank foundations are neither membership-based nor owner-based organizations. They are characterized by an internal organizational structure, stable funds, and assets.

Bank foundations have a nearly permanent identity and purpose based on an original deed represented by a statute. This basis establishes their purposes, organizational structures, and activities to carry out.

Bank foundations are separate from government or public agencies. They often promote and implement initiatives together with the government and other public agencies. However, they are private and, as such, are not directly controlled by the government and are structurally separate from public agencies.

Bank foundations govern themselves. They are autonomous entities equipped to control their own activities; they have their own internal governance procedures and a separate set of accounts.

Bank foundations are not profit-distributing entities, and they do not operate on the basis of profit-oriented motivations. By provision of the law, any surplus of revenue must be applied to its social mission.

Bank foundations serve a public purpose. They do not serve the needs of a narrow social group but instead use their financial resources for public benefit.

There are also a few unique differences specific to Italian bank foundations compared with foundations in general. One of the main differences is their historical origin. Bank foundations derived from rapid recent developments following autocratic experience (Anheier 2001). They were not founded by an individual, group of individuals, family, or company bringing private assets into the foundation. Instead, they arose simultaneously in the 1990s by law, relying on assets obtained from public savings banks rather than donations or fundraisers.

The law dictates their social purpose and prescribes their mission, and as such, these aspects of the foundation are not voluntary in nature. The law states that bank foundations must pursue exclusively socially oriented aims and promote economic development in accordance with their individual statutes. Each bank foundation can then choose the sectors in which to carry out its activities among those permitted by law.

As private entities that perform on behalf of the public interest (Amorosino 2009), they are legally constrained in terms of the use of their assets and the resulting incomes (Sala 2010). The operating surplus has to be partially allocated to reserves. The remainder must be assigned to the institutional activity that can take place only in a list of permitted sectors.

1.3 Governance in Bank Foundations

Governance is the system of relations among the board, management, and auditors, and it defines the way organizations are directed and managed to accomplish their mission and objectives. The distribution of rights and responsibilities among different entities in the organization, such as the board, managers, and stakeholders, and the rules and procedures of decision making constitute the elements of the governance structure (Anheier 2005).

Nonprofit governance is highly diverse due to the wide differences among nonprofit organizations in terms of mission and sources on which they depend (Young 2011). A good governance needs to fit the specific characteristics of the organization. In this sense, Anheier (2005) observes that the number of bottom lines in a nonprofit organization will change in relation to its mission, objectives, task environment, organizational structure, and the number of stakeholders.

A bottom line that is relevant in talking about bank foundations' governance is that regarding the dual governance–management structure (Anheier 2005). The dual governance model separates the board from management within a nonprofit organization. The board is in charge of laying out the mission, defining objectives and strategies, and developing programs, while management provides an executive function (Middleton 1987) and focuses on operational aspects and financial matters in running the organization (Anheier 2005).

Prior literature has highlighted that the balance of power between board and management is affected by three type of variables: individual (e.g., gender, prestige of board members), organizational (e.g., size, age), and environmental (e.g., organizational financial dependence on board members, stability, governmental funding) (Ostrower and Stone 2006).

Pointer and Orlikoff (2002) emphasize that the most important decision about governance that the board assumes is where to draw the boundary between board and management work, to avoid the perception that the board has abdicated its responsibilities. Such responsibilities consist of defining the objectives to be pursued and verifying the results achieved. In contrast, management is in charge of carrying out the operations through which the programs put forth by the board can be realized.

The foundation's governance structure derives its impetus from the need to use assets assigned by the owner for public purposes. The relationship between the owner (or donor) and the board is defined by the mission given to the foundation and the assets assigned to the organization. The board is responsible for setting objectives, strategies, and programs in line with achieving a social purpose. The relationship between board and management then is depicted by a dual governance model. Specifically, management is responsible for the proper use of assets within the programs defined by the board.

Italian bank foundations differ somewhat from this model due to their particular nature. While the dual model provides for a deep separation between the board, which determines strategic functions, and management, which executes the actions, the governance structure of Italian bank foundations is more articulated (Fig. 1.1).

As Fig. 1.1 shows, there are two boards with different but complementary functions in a bank foundation. The Board of Trustees represents the body in charge of the foundation's direction and strategic function. It is responsible for defining objectives, strategies, and long-term programs in the exclusive interest of the territory in which the foundation operates. The Board of Directors is in charge of the administrative function, and it is responsible for implementing the bank foundation's strategy. The Board of Directors is appointed by the Board of Trustees, but it is not a mere executor of its guidelines. The Board of Directors has the more complex duty of translating the long-term programs into short-term plans of action for management to implement at the operational level. In addition, the Board of Directors can formulate proposals to the Board of Trustees.

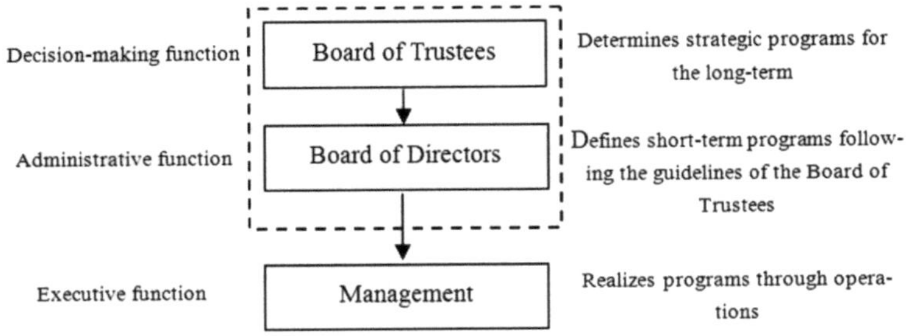

Fig. 1.1 Governance structure model for Italian bank foundations

Therefore, the Board of Directors, through the definition of short-term programs, completes the strategic planning activity designed by the Board of Trustees. In this way, it embodies a connection between the policy-making body and management, allowing the foundation to overcome one of the main criticisms of the dual governance model for nonprofit organizations.

As a result of the presence of two boards, the Board of Trustees has many components and can represent a significant part of the interests that insist on the bank foundation. In this regard, literature highlights that the board does not represent the ownership that transferred the assets to the organization. Rather, it is a body that represents the foundation and is responsible for identifying and meeting the needs of the territory in which it operates (Anheier 2005; DuBois et al. 2009). As Gill (2005, p. 24) argues, the board must "represent the organization and its programs positively to key stakeholders and the community at large."

The Board of Trustees therefore plays a key role in the relationship between the foundation and its stakeholders. Thus, it is important that the organization adopts a multistakeholder approach in choosing the members of its governance bodies.

References

ACRI (2013) Diciottesimo rapporto sulle fondazioni di origine bancaria. Rome

Amorosino S (2009) Le fondazioni di origine bancaria tra potere pubblico e autonomia privata: ipotesi sul futuribile. Il Risparmio 1(1):77–88

Andrews FE (1956) Philanthropic foundations. Russell Sage, New York

Anheier HK (2001) Foundations in Europe: a comparative perspective. In: Schülter A, Then V, Walkenhorst P (eds) Foundations in Europe: society, management and law. Directory of Social Change, London, pp 35–81

Anheier HK (2005) Nonprofit organizations: theory, management, policy. Routledge, London/ New York

De Andrés-Alonso P, Azofra-Palenzuela V, Romero-Merino ME (2009) Determinants of nonprofit board size and composition: the case of Spanish foundations. Nonprof Volunt Sec Q 38:784–809

Diaz WA (1996) The behavior of foundations in an organizational frame: a case study. Nonprof Volunt Sec Q 25:453–469

Drucker PF (1990) Managing the non-profit organization: principles and practices. HarperCollins, New York

DuBois C, Caers R, Jegers M, De Cooman R, De Gieter S, Pepermans R (2009) Agency conflicts between board and manager a discrete choice experiment in Flemish nonprofit schools. Nonprofit Manag Leadersh 20(2):165–183

European Foundation Centre (2003) Typology of foundations in Europe. Brussels

European Foundation Centre (2005) Foundation facts & figures across the EU—associating private wealth for public benefit. Brussels

Gill MD (2005) Governing for results: a director's guide to good governance. Trafford, Victoria

Handy C (1990) Understanding voluntary organizations: how to make them function effectively. Penguin, London

Hudson M (1999) Managing without profit: the art of managing third-sector organizations. Penguin, London

Middleton M (1987) Nonprofit boards of directors: beyond the governance function. In: Powell WW (ed) The nonprofit sector: a research handbook. Yale University Press, New Haven, pp 141–153

Ostrower F, Stone MM (2006) Governance: research trends, gaps, and future prospects. In: Powell WW, Steinberg RS (eds) The nonprofit sector: a research handbook, 2nd edn. Yale University Press, New Haven/London, pp 612–628

Pointer DD, Orlikoff JE (2002) The high performance board: principles of nonprofit organization governance. Jossey-Bass, San Francisco

Sala GA (2010) La vocazione delle fondazioni bancarie nell'arte e nella cultura. In: Leardini C, Rossi G (eds) Fondazioni bancarie, arte e cultura. Franco Angeli, Milan, pp 17–25

Salamon LM, Anheier HK (1992) In search of the nonprofit sector I: the question of definitions. Voluntas 3(2):125–151

Young DR (2011) The prospective role of economic stakeholders in the governance of nonprofit organizations. Voluntas 22:566–586

Chapter 2
Outlining Italian Bank Foundations

2.1 When the Origin Makes the Difference

In Italy, the number of nonprofit organizations has grown significantly in the past 20 years. Most of this change and expansion has been a result of the emergence of bank foundations, defined in general as nonprofit groups with their own income and governing boards that use their financial resources for public benefit (European Foundation Centre 2003, 2005).

The appearance of bank foundations in the Italian economic landscape has not been spontaneous but rather been the result of a deep legislative process of reform involving the Italian banking system during the 1990s. The legal origin of these organizations has affected their aims as well as the procedures for carrying out their activities. At the same time, it has given them some characteristics that make Italian bank foundations unique compared with foundations in general.

2.1.1 The Origin by Law

Italian bank foundations are a recent phenomenon. They were developed in the 1990s as a result of a legislative process aimed at privatizing and modernizing the public banking system (Emmanuele 2004).

They did not arise from a private sector initiative but rather were the result of a series of legal reforms that began with the Amato Laws (Law no. 218/90 and Decree no. 356/90). As such, they represent an act of "social engineering" (Zamagni 2007).

Before the passage of these laws, the Italian credit system was characterized by the presence of public savings banks that began in the nineteenth century, initiated either by the state or by individuals (Bruni 1999). As a priority, these banks primarily engaged in lending activities. However, given their public origin, they

C. Leardini et al., *Board Governance in Bank Foundations*, Contributions to Management Science, DOI 10.1007/978-3-642-41306-3_2,

also pursued social purposes to demonstrate a philanthropic attitude (Salamon and Anheier 1997), donating a part of their profits to public interest initiatives.

With the Amato Laws in the early 1990s, the philanthropic activities of the banks were separated from the credit functions to ensure a greater efficiency in the banking system. More specifically, the credit business was "spun off" from the public banks, which in turn maintained only philanthropic activity. The two activities, originally carried out jointly within the public banks, were therefore assigned permanently to separate and distinct entities that took the place of the original public savings banks: "spin-off" banks on one hand and bank foundations on the other.

As a result of the reform, new banks in the form of joint stock companies began to spring up, and these entities pursued a profit intent. The credit business was entrusted exclusively to these entities, facilitating in this way the reorganization of the Italian banking system. At the same time, the number of foundations in Italy increased dramatically due to the proliferation of bank foundations—a new kind of nonprofit organization charged solely with philanthropic activity.

Although the spin-off banks and the foundations are separate and distinct entities, a participatory relationship exists that link the two organizations. The shares of the new spin-off banks are controlled in large part by the bank foundations. Together with other forms of capital investments, the spin-off banks aim to increase shareholder wealth, which in this case effectively provides the funds necessary for the foundations to carry out their philanthropic activity.

It follows then that the members of bank foundations' boards cannot have management roles in the banks of which they are shareholders.

Shareholding in Spin-Off Banks

After their origin in the early 1990s, bank foundations were required to maintain majority ownership of the spin-off banks. For some years, they were almost the exclusive trustees of the capital derived from the new privatized banks.

This link with the banking sector lost some of its strength with a new reform. The first step of this new reform was Law no. 474/94, which eliminated this requirement and favoured instead the investment diversification of bank foundations. A second and more significant step was Law no. 461/98 (also known as the Ciampi Law). The foundations were required to relinquish any control in the spin-off banks, with the exception of foundations with a book value of net assets less than €200 million or those located in special statue regions. The obligation is still in force today.

The situation at the end of the 2012 was as follows (ACRI 2013):

Foundations with shares in the spin-off bank >50 %		13
Foundations without shares in the spin-off bank		22
Foundations with shares in the spin-off bank <50 %		53
Less than 5 %	22	

(continued)

(continued)

Between 5 % and 20 %	17
Between 21 % and 50 %	14
Total of foundations	**88**

2.1.2 *The Exclusive Purpose of Promoting Social and Economic Development*

Under the law, bank foundations were designated the exclusive purpose of promoting social and economic development of the territory, beyond a profit-making intent.

Although foundation law underwent major reforms (Basile 2003), the socially oriented role of bank foundations has never been questioned. In particular, Article 2 of Legislative Decree no. 153/99 reiterated that a bank foundation is a private legal person with statutory and management autonomy, pursuing only objectives of social and economic development of the territory. They are allowed neither the exercise of business activities nor the performance of credit functions. They are also excluded from any form of financing, disbursement, or subsidy involving entities with a profit intent.

The attribution of public purposes to bank foundations must, however, be properly understood. It does not prevent foundations from carrying out activities other than those of a social nature. Rather, it requires that such activities be instrumental to the public interest objectives that foundations pursue. Therefore, asset management and participation in banks or companies, for example, are not contradictory to institutional purposes if their aim is to produce a gain that helps meet social goals. It also follows that returns on investments must be used as a means to achieve the statutory purposes.

In this way, the philanthropic aim that used to be secondary for public banks has become the main purpose of bank foundations (Merusi 2002). They have become independent organizations with their own assets and statutory and management autonomy, in the service of public utilities (Danzi and Demarie 2003).

2.1.3 *Asset Management for Grant-Making Activity*

The characteristics of the business are influenced by the particular nature of bank foundations: They are private legal entities, autonomous and self-governed, with their own assets managed in a nonspeculative way that operate without profit intent for the satisfaction of the general interests of the territory (Zagrebelsky 2009).

Bank foundations have inherited the vast assets of public savings banks, which need to be managed in an efficient way. At the same time, bank foundations are nonprofit entities in the exclusive pursuit of social purposes and have the legal obligation to use their proceeds to finance activities involving aims of general utility.

Their business comprises two major areas of activity: asset management activity, aimed at maximizing the return on investment, and grant-making activity, focused on the maximization of value for the territory (Alberti 2002; Leardini 2005; Tieghi 2002).

The distinction between asset management and grant-making activity is suggested by the law, which states that asset management must be carried out with organizational procedures suitable for ensuring its separation from the other activities of the foundation.

Although asset management and grant-making activity are both important, the core business of bank foundations is the grant-making activity. As established by law and reaffirmed by the statutes, bank foundations engage mainly in socially oriented and economic development undertakings. The management of assets therefore is functional and instrumental to grant-making activity.

The Statutes

Fondazione Cassa di Risparmio di Verona Vicenza Belluno e Ancona

Article 2: The Foundation inspires its work for the common good and pursues exclusively socially oriented aims and promotion of economic development, ensuring the balanced allocation of funds with preference to areas with greater social relevance. To this end, the Foundation operates in the areas allowed by law.

Article 5: The Foundation's assets consist of financial assets (shares, bonds, bank deposits, etc.), movable property, and estate assets (furniture, equipment, etc.), and it is totally committed to the pursuit of institutional goals and managed consistent with the nature of the Foundation as a nonprofit organization that operates according to principles of transparency and morality.

Bank foundations use financial resources to satisfy the needs of the territory in which they operate (Tieghi 1995). To this end, they support own projects and social initiatives carried out by third parties that promote social and economic development. The main lever through which bank foundations realize their mission is grants—that is, donations or nonrepayable subsidies disbursed to private nonprofit organizations or public institutions.

Grant-making activity requires the foundation to know the needs of the stakeholders and their order of priority, to identify actions that will satisfy these needs, and to find the funds necessary to implement the interventions.

The funds delivered to the territory derive from asset management. In particular, the funds represent a part of the operating surplus—that is, total revenues and gains net of costs and taxes—after assignments to reserves (e.g., mandatory reserve, value fluctuation reserve), the fulfilment of legal obligations, and the repayment of any previous deficit.

Asset management is therefore closely linked to grant-making activity (Cioccarelli and Previtali 2002). Regarding the former, net assets are invested to obtain the funds needed to finance interventions. Regarding the latter, the funds are then used within the specific areas of intervention chosen by the foundation.

The same law (Article 7 of Legislative Decree no. 153/1999) requires that asset investments ensure the most appropriate connection with the institutional purposes of the foundation. It means that asset management is bound by the needs of the grant-making activity and is not independent from it.

This functional link also highlights a temporal connection between asset management and grant-making activity. The two activities are not simultaneous but rather are successive to each other.

As Fig. 2.1 shows, asset management is an activity that logically and chronologically precedes grant-making activity. Operating surplus produced by the management of a foundation's assets in period t provides the financial resources necessary in the next period (t + 1) to carry out interventions of social utility through grant-making activity.

In the management of assets, bank foundations use available financial resources to buy securities, make equity investments, invest in property, and so forth. Article 7 of Legislative Decree no. 153/1999 puts constraints on investment decisions. Bank foundations must abide by the following:

- They must diversify the risk of their investment portfolio.
- They must strive to achieve a return on investments that is consistent with the requirements of the grant-making activity.

The income derived from the trading of financial instruments and their return in the form of interest and dividends must, first, cover the operating costs. The operating surplus that remains is partially reinvested in asset management to maintain the integrity of the capital. The surplus is then used to carry out the grant-making activity.

The allocation of operating surplus is the starting point of the grant-making activity and represents the connection between institutional activity and asset management.

The tight correlation between the asset management and grant-making activities requires careful planning and a strategic coordination by a single body with a unitary view (Salamon and Voytek 1989). The investment decisions made under the asset management function must take into account the needs arising from the grant-making activity. Conversely, the grant-making activity cannot be separated from the return on investment of the asset management function, because it is financially dependent on the successful management of the assets.

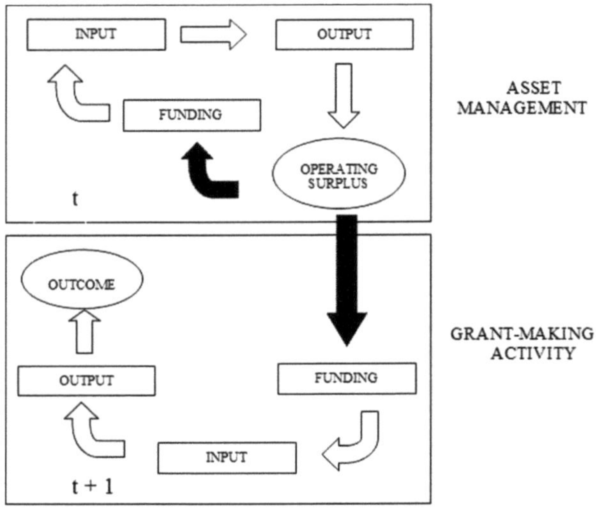

Fig. 2.1 Relationship between asset management and grant-making activity

2.2 Size and Geographic Distribution

As of December 31, 2012 (ACRI 2013), there were 88 bank foundations in Italy that varied widely in terms of their size and geographic distribution, with a total book value of net assets amounting to €42 billion and 1,023 full-time employees (on average, 11.6 people per foundation).

The size is established by the total amount of net assets. To show this phenomenon, Table 2.1 divides Italian bank foundations into five groups similar in number, using the criterion of statistical quintiles (ACRI 2013).

Table 2.1 shows a high concentration of net assets. The 18 large bank foundations represent 73.7 % of the total net assets, while the 18 smallest ones hold only accounted for 1.6 %.

With regard to the geographic distribution, foundations are generally grouped according to the four traditional geographical divisions of the country: northwest, northeast, central, and south and islands (Fig. 2.2).

The number of foundations varies significantly by geographical area. As Table 2.2 shows, 60 of the 88 foundations are located in the northeast and the central regions of the country. Only 11 are located in the south and islands, though this region has an almost equal reach.

Their non-homogeneous presence within the country derives from the distribution of the original savings banks from which the foundations arose. These savings banks were widespread in both northern and central Italy and almost entirely absent in the south.

By observing the distribution of net assets in terms of size and geographic area, it seems clear that the Italian bank foundation system is characterized by a significant degree of concentration.

Table 2.1 Number and size of Italian bank foundations (ACRI 2013)

Size	Number	Net assets (€)	% of total net assets
Large bank foundations	18	31,076,041,150	73.7
Medium-large bank foundations	17	5,654,491,350	13.4
Medium bank foundations	18	3,044,446,349	7.2
Medium-small bank foundations	17	1,725,939,348	4.1
Small bank foundations	18	682,121,805	1.6
Total	**88**	**42,183,240,002**	**100**

Fig. 2.2 Geographic distribution of Italian bank foundations (http://www.acri.it)

In the north of the country, 47 foundations are in operation, with net assets of more than €31 billion (74.7 % of the total). Among them, the large-sized foundations have more than half of the total net assets (€31,077 million of the €42,183 million). In the northwest region, the average net assets are more than twice the average

Table 2.2 Net assets distribution by size and geographic area (ACRI 2013)

	Small		Medium-small		Medium		Medium-large		Large		Total		
	Millions of Euros	N	Millions of Euros	N	Millions of Euros	N	Millions of Euros	N	Millions of Euros	N	Millions of Euros	N	Average
Northwest	155	4	112	1	584	3	750	3	17,224	6	18,825	17	1,107
Northeast	118	5	450	4	965	6	2,723	8	8,419	7	12,675	30	423
Central	337	7	636	7	1,195	7	1,971	5	4,559	4	8,698	30	290
South and islands	72	2	528	5	300	2	210	1	875	1	1,985	11	181
Total	**682**	**18**	**1,726**	**17**	**3,044**	**18**	**5,654**	**17**	**31,077**	**18**	**42,183**	**88**	**479**
Average	38		102		169		333		1,727		479		

Table 2.3 Asset composition (ACRI 2013)

	2012			2011		
Assets	Millions of Euros		%	Millions of Euros		%
Property investments and intangible assets		1,869.0	3.7		1,828.9	3.4
Financial assets		46,863.3	91.9		49,737.2	94.2
Investments in spin-off banks	20,199.8		39.6	21,053.7		39.9
Investments in other companies	4,755.2		9.3	5,062.4		9.6
Investments in instrumental enterprises	907.8		1.8	847.2		1.6
Other financial assets	21,000.5		41.2	22,773.9		43.1
Receivables		627.1	1.2		465.4	0.9
Cash and cash equivalents		1,544.5	3.0		676.4	1.3
Other assets		97.7	0.2		97.8	0.2
Total Assets		51,001.6	100.0		52,805.6	100.0

(€1,107 million of the €479 million), while in southern Italy and the islands, the average (€181 million) is less than half of the total system.

As a result of the different size and geographical distribution, a smaller volume of institutional activity is allocated to southern Italy.

2.3 Assets

The funds to be disbursed to the territory derive mainly from the management of foundations' assets. Asset composition is extremely diversified. A synthesis of the main items that compose them appears in Table 2.3.

The total assets of Italian bank foundations (€51 billion) consist of approximately 96 % financial assets. Only 3.7 % is represented by property investments and intangible assets. This is consistent with the notion that foundations do not play a production activity in a narrow sense but rather invest in diverse interest-bearing activities (e.g., financial instruments, banking investments).

Regarding the duration of the investments, approximately 66 % of financial assets are long-term financial investments (€34 billion), while short-term financial assets amount to approximately €12.8 billion.

Both types of investments have undergone significant downsizing that is not related to a reduction of the grant-making activity. Final assets have undergone a significant reduction due to the need for cash to fund capital increases in the spin-off banks. The interconnections between the spin-off banks and bank foundations thus are still relevant.

Table 2.4 Composition of revenues and gains by type (ACRI 2013)

	2012 (%)	2011 (%)
Spin-off bank dividends	29.1	54.7
Other dividends and interests	46.1	36
Gains and losses of financial instruments	6.9	−43.5
Extraordinary incomes and expenses	17.9	52.8
Total	**100**	**100**

Support for Spin-Off Banks

During 2012, bank foundations provided capital increases to the spin-off banks totalling €1.2 billion.

In addition, they gave up the dividends and subscribed to the convertible debenture loans issued by the major Italian banks.

In this way, bank foundations have continued to support the spin-off banks in moments of great difficulty by allowing them to comply with the capital ratios required by the European Banking Authority. This intervention was enacted to avoid the possibility that banks would have to neglect enterprises and households in terms of credit support.

Since the inception of the international financial crisis in 2008, bank foundations have provided the major national banks with €8.6 billion.

The financial assets in which bank foundations invest their capital are interest-bearing activities that produce a diverse set of revenues and gains. Table 2.4 shows the evolution of the composition of the revenues and gains during the 2011–2012 period.

In 2012, the total ordinary revenues and gains amounted to €1,535.6 million, an increase of 24.1 % compared with the amount from the previous year (ACRI 2013). The return on net assets (ratio of ordinary revenues and gains, net after withholding taxes, to the book value of net assets) went from 2.7 % in 2011 to 3.6 % in 2012 (see Table 2.5).

Dividends and interest earned on investments other than the spin-off banks represented the main source of bank foundations' income (46.1 % of total revenues). Dividends paid by the spin-off banks decreased significantly (€445 million in 2012, €677 million in 2011), though the return on these shares did not change much (2.3 % in 2012, 2.9 % in 2011).

Ordinary and extraordinary incomes and expenses constituted the remaining 17.9 % of the total revenues. This value decreased significantly in 2012, compared with the previous year.

The operating surplus for 2012 amounted to €1,069.7 million, reflecting a significant increase compared with the amount from the previous year (€470.6 million). A part of this surplus was assigned to mandatory reserves. The remaining has been allocated to philanthropic activities.

Table 2.5 Return on assets (ACRI 2013)

	2012 (%)	2011 (%)
Return on net assets	3.6	2.7
Return on financial assets	2.8	−0.3
Return on spin-off banks investments	2.3	2.9

For more information, Appendix (see Sects. A.1 and A.2) provides the relevant financial statement items for Italian bank foundations, focusing on 2011 and 2012.

2.4 Areas and Manner of Intervention in Grant-Making Activity

The operating surplus deriving from asset management activity is used to support activities of collective interest within the eligible sectors designated by the law. The main form of intervention is represented by grants and disbursements, in the form of money that bank foundations allocate to own or third-party projects that have been deemed to be a priority in the interests of local territory.

The reduction in returns of the asset management function, which is the main lever through which the bank foundations achieve their mission, has reduced the total funds available to the grant-making activity. Bank foundations, however, have maintained a high level of disbursements thanks to the efficiency of the management and the ability to draw on the vast reserves they have accumulated over the years to cope in the event of crisis.

In 2012, total funds allocated to grant-making activities amounted to €965.8 million. The number of projects financed reached 22,204, with an average amount per project of €43,496. The rate of grant-making in 2012, calculated in terms of average net assets, was 2.3 %, as in previous year. The total disbursements decreased by 11.6 % compared with the previous year due to the continuing economic crisis.

The reduction was significant but limited due to the use of funds prudently accumulated by foundations during the previous years and allocated to reserves to cope with difficult situations such as the economic crisis.

Table 2.6 shows the allocation of grants by size and geographic distribution of bank foundations.

In addition to the net assets, disbursements are also concentrated in the hands of a few foundations. In 2012, the 18 major foundations alone paid 75.2 % of the available funds, with 41.8 % of the total interventions. In contrast, small foundations provided only 1.6 % of the total funds allocated to the grant-making activity.

The same relationship between net assets and grants is evident in geographic distribution. Again, the foundations located in the south and islands region show the smallest volume of institutional activity.

Table 2.6 The distribution of grants for Italian bank foundations (ACRI 2013)

	2012	
Foundation	Amount of grants (%)	Number of interventions (%)
Size		
Large	75.2	41.8
Medium-large	13.5	18.8
Medium	6.3	19.8
Medium-small	3.4	10.4
Small	1.6	9.2
Total	**100**	**100**
Geographic distribution		
Northwest	42.9	34.0
Northeast	30.3	31.5
Central	23.0	23.6
South and islands	3.8	10.9
Total	**100**	**100**

2.4.1 Sectors of Intervention

Bank foundations direct their activities exclusively in the areas admitted by law (Article 1 of Legislative Decree no. 153/1999) and give preference to areas with greater social relevance for the territory in which they operate. Each foundation indicates in its statute the relevant sectors in which it preferentially allocates its funds, as well as the other areas in which it has decided to operate.

The choice of sectors for operations highlights the tendency toward a high degree of specialization. Italian bank foundations concentrate more than 70 % of their total funding in four sectors, reflecting the provisions of the law, which requires that foundations allocate the available funds to no more than five significant sectors. The average number of sectors for each foundation is seven (ACRI 2013).

As Table 2.7 shows, most of the grants go to arts and culture, education, social assistance, and research.

2.4.1.1 Art, Cultural Activities, and Heritage

As in previous years, the main sector that receives the allocated funds is art, cultural activities, and heritage, garnering 31.6 % of the total funding in 2012 for a total of €305.3 million. Culture has consistently been a significant area of intervention for bank foundations (Leardini and Rossi 2010). All 88 Italian bank foundations work in this sector. They invest in art, cultural activities, and heritage with the explicit recognition that they are operating in a country whose historical, artistic, and cultural heritage is very important (ACRI 2013).

Table 2.7 Distribution of grants by sector (ACRI 2013)

	2012				2011			
Sectors	Millions of Euros	%	Number of interventions	%	Millions of Euros	%	Number of interventions	%
Art, cultural activities, and heritage	305.3	31.6	7,872	35.5	335.4	30.7	9,179	36.9
Education, learning, and training	144.8	15.0	3,427	15.4	127.0	11.6	4,032	16.2
Social assistance	124.5	12.9	2,712	12.2	152.7	14.0	2,766	11.1
Research	118.5	12.3	1,244	5.6	156.3	14.3	1,506	6.0
Volunteering, philanthropy and charity	117.3	12.1	2,682	12.1	99.2	9.1	2,858	11.5
Local development	55.4	5.7	1,379	6.2	50.0	4.6	1,451	5.8
Health	54.6	5.7	1,129	5.1	103.6	9.5	1,048	4.2
Environmental protection and quality	18.4	1.9	354	1.6	27.7	2.5	426	1.7
Family	17.4	1.8	218	1.0	27.0	2.5	346	1.4
Sport and recreation	8.6	0.9	1,117	4.9	12.7	1.2	1,220	4.9
Crime prevention and public safety	0.4	0.1	17	0.1	0.2	0.0	14	0.1
Civil rights	0.3	0.0	35	0.2	0.3	0.0	25	0.1
Religion	0.2	0.0	18	0.1	0.5	0.0	35	0.1
Total	**965.8**	**100.0**	**22,204**	**100.0**	**1,092.5**	**100.0**	**24,906**	**100.0**

Table 2.8 Composition of disbursements to arts and culture (ACRI 2013)

	2012			
Subarea of intervention	Millions of Euros	%	Number of interventions	%
Conservation and enhancement of architectural and archaeological heritage	83.7	27.4	974	12.4
Artistic and literary creation and interpretation	80.6	26.4	2,101	26.7
Museums activities	31.4	10.3	376	4.8
Visual arts	14.9	4.9	345	4.4
Libraries and archives	6.2	2.0	212	2.7
Publishing and other means of mass communication	5.8	1.9	382	4.9
Other cultural and artistic activities	35.7	11.7	2,335	29.7
Not classified	46.9	15.4	1,147	14.4
Total	**305.3**	**100.0**	**7,872**	**100.0**

Table 2.8 shows the composition of disbursements that go to the art and culture subareas of intervention.

As Table 2.8 highlights, bank foundations operate mainly to conserve and enhance Italy's architectural and archaeological heritage, through the restoration of historical centers, urban renewal, and other restoration efforts. More than 27 % of the funds available for the sector were allocated to this subarea (€83.7 million of the €305.3 million).

Another important subarea is represented by initiatives to support the creation and interpretation of art and literature. These disbursements go to private individuals who engage in various forms of artistic expression, such as music, dance, theater, and literature. Bank foundations allocate an average of 26 % of their art and culture funds to this area.

The remainder of the funds goes to activities, visual arts, libraries and archives, publishing and other means of mass communication, and other residual cultural and artistic activities.

2.4.1.2 Education, Learning, and Training

Since their initiation, bank foundations have financed and promoted education, learning and training initiatives. They complement public action and serve a key function in promoting and implementing relevant initiatives, in cooperation with the government and public administrations.

As of the end of 2012, the education sector was the second most funded area, receiving €144.8 million (15.0 % of the total). Table 2.9 shows the composition of disbursements that go to the education-related subareas of intervention.

University education has consistently been a significant area of intervention for bank foundations. In 2012, it represented the main subarea within the sector, with

Table 2.9 Composition of disbursements to education, learning and training (ACRI 2013)

	2012			
Subareas of intervention	Millions of Euros	%	Number of interventions	%
University education	52.4	36.2	391	11.4
Primary and secondary school education	35.7	24.6	1,474	43.0
Professional training	24.1	16.7	417	12.2
Young education	8.8	6.1	478	13.9
Not classified	23.8	16.4	667	19.5
Total	**144.8**	**100.0**	**3,427**	**100.0**

€52.4 million (36.2 % of the amounts allocated to the sector). Primary and secondary school education, involving 1,474 projects, received €35.7 million.

2.4.1.3 Social Assistance

In 2012, social assistance was the third sector of intervention, receiving €124.5 million (12.9 % of the allocated funds).

The name of this field is intentionally broad. It includes several lines of action through which foundations support citizens in conditions of difficulty or at risk of social exclusion: integration of the disabled, protection for the non-self-sufficient elderly, child protection, and recovery and reintegration for the most socially disadvantaged people exposed to forms of marginalization and abuse. Working in this sector, bank foundations implement the principle of horizontal subsidiarity provided for by the Italian Constitution. Their funding does not replace state intervention but rather cooperates with public and private entities to carry out integrated projects that are of importance to the local community.

Table 2.10 shows the composition of disbursements that go to social assistance subareas of intervention.

Within this sector, the main subarea of intervention is represented by social services, garnering 90 % of the total amount paid in the sector. In most cases, these services help disabled people (42.7 %), the elderly (19.6 %), and children (14.5 %) in the capacity of home services, host infrastructures, and measures to support families, among other activities (ACRI 2013).

Civil protection services and assistance to refugees and displaced people cover the remaining 3.6 % of the total grants in the social assistance sector.

2.4.1.4 Research

As of the end of 2012, the research sector was the fourth-most funded area, with €118.5 million (12.3 % of the total). The commitment of the foundations to the research sector has been reflected in various areas of intervention.

Table 2.11 shows the composition of disbursements that go to subareas of the research sector.

Table 2.10 Composition of disbursements to social assistance (ACRI 2013)

	2012			
Subarea of intervention	Millions of Euros	%	Number of interventions	%
Social services	112.0	90.0	2,178	80.3
Civil protection, assistance to refugees and displaced persons	4.4	3.6	178	6.6
Not classified	8.0	6.4	356	13.1
Total	124.5	100.0	2,712	100.0

Table 2.11 Composition of disbursements to research (ACRI 2013)

	2012			
Subareas of intervention	Millions of Euros	%	Number of interventions	%
Natural sciences and technology	35.8	30.2	285	22.9
Research and development in the medical field	14.8	12.5	164	13.2
Research in the field of social sciences	3.3	2.8	147	11.8
Other research fields	33.9	28.6	440	35.4
Not classified	30.6	25.9	208	16.7
Total	**118.5**	**100.0**	**1,244**	**100.0**

Among the specific fields of research, 30.2 % of the funds went to the subarea of natural sciences and technology. Following this, research and development in the medical field and research in the field of social sciences received 12.5 % and 2.8 %, respectively, of the amounts allocated to this sector.

The most common types of intervention in the sector (62.2 % of the funds provided in 2012) are funding of specific projects at research institutions, both public and private (ACRI 2013).

2.4.2 *Manner of Intervention*

In general, foundations operate in different forms and have different ways to answer the needs of individuals and socioeconomic territory.

According to the usual distinction proposed in literature (Anheier 2001; Bulmer 1999; Karl and Katz 1987; McCarthy 1989), foundations may be classified as grant-making or operating foundations. In the former case, they are gift givers that deliver financial contributions to a third party; in the latter case, they directly define and implement projects and programs and assume responsibility for project design, planning, and operational implementation of their own projects.

Such modalities of interventions are often mixed within the same foundation, although it is possible to identify a prevalence of a particular kind. Anheier (2005) highlights that in Austria, Belgium, Norway, and Turkey, the majority of foundations are of a mixed type; in France, Greece, and Spain, operating foundations are the dominant type; and in Canada, Britain, Germany, the Netherlands, and the United States, grant-making foundations are the dominant type.

As foundations in general, Italian bank foundations may have a diverse morphology. In the initial phase of development, Italian bank foundations were grant-making institutions. After the separation of the credit business from philanthropic activities, they essentially became charities that disbursed contributions to those who required them.

The grant-making model presents a set of advantages extremely useful for these new entities (Tieghi 1995): It requires minimal organizational structure, and it is not necessary to make considerable investments.

Even now, the grant-making activity is still prevalent in Italian bank foundations, but with some "corrections" compared with the past. First, funding is allocated after careful selection of applications, especially in light of the possible impact on socioeconomic development. Second, bank foundations are more involved in the definition of strategic and programmatic elements of third-party projects.

At the same time, however, the number of own projects has increased, becoming a priority point of action for bank foundations (Boesso et al. 2011). This changing model highlights the proactive role that foundations play within a territory (Anheier 2001). In this way, the foundation develops a sort of entrepreneurial management style and a high degree of expertise (Anheier and Leat 2002), which favors diffusion of an entrepreneurial culture (Beyer 1999; Leat 1999) within bank foundations.

Despite the prevalence of grant-making activity over operating activities, Italian bank foundations' typical manner of intervention is an integrated mix of the two approaches (grant-making and operating). It should also be noted that bank foundations can operate in a third way, through instrumental enterprises. These are companies carried by foundations that operate exclusively for the direct implementation of the statutory purposes in the relevant sectors. Although foundations, in general, may not engage in business activities, exceptions are made in such cases when business activity is strictly instrumental to the achievement of institutional goals in the relevant sectors.

As Table 2.12 shows, grant-making activity in 2012 remains the prevalent model (86.3 % of total disbursements in 2012) and is more prevalent in large-sized foundations (90.6 %). In contrast, small-sized foundations tend to engage in the largest number of own projects (21.5 % compared with an average of 9.4 %). Instrumental enterprises prevail in medium- to large-sized foundations (15.2 % compared with an average of 4.3 %).

Projects directly controlled by the foundations thus have increased in amount (9.4 % in 2012, 7.9 % in 2011) and contribute to support organizations that already are operating in the community.

Table 2.12 Funding by size and manner of intervention (ACRI 2013)

	2012		
Foundations	Grant making (%)	Own projects (%)	Instrumental enterprises (%)
Large	90.6	7.1	2.3
Medium-large	65.2	19.6	15.2
Medium	87.4	10.6	2.0
Medium-small	78.8	14.0	7.2
Small	72.2	21.5	6.3
Total	**86.3**	**9.4**	**4.3**

Table 2.13 Funding by size and involvement of other parties (ACRI 2013)

	2012	
Foundation	Individual disbursements (%)	Pooled disbursements (%)
Large	84.5	15.5
Medium-large	94.6	5.4
Medium	87.3	12.7
Medium-small	93.3	6.7
Small	94.9	5.1
Total	**86.6**	**13.4**

2.4.3 Collaboration with Other Entities

Bank foundations can operate autonomously or in partnership with other organizations (pooled disbursements). Such partnerships can take on various combinations of local, public, and private actors, which increases the value generated by their action and gives rise to significant synergies.

These partnerships combine the interests and funds of different entities and favor the development of articulated and wide-ranging projects. During the past few years, particular emphasis has been placed on long-term projects realized in conjunction with other bank foundations, favoring a process of rationalization of interventions. Table 2.13 highlights the distribution of projects, along with the involvement of other parties in 2012.

In 2012, 13.4 % of the total projects involved bank foundations and other entities such as government, religious institutions, nonprofit organizations, and foundations. Large foundations in particular collaborated with other organizations, providing 15.5 % of their funds to pooled disbursements. In the most common cases (39.6 % of cases), the partners are public institutions (ACRI 2013).

2.4.4 Beneficiaries

The ultimate recipients of bank foundations' activities are citizens. However, they are not the direct beneficiaries of the foundations' grants. These funds are assigned

Table 2.14 Funding by beneficiaries type in 2012 (ACRI 2013)

	Private sector			Public sector		
Foundation	Foundations (%)	Associations (%)	Other private entities (%)	Non territorial public entities (%)	Local authorities (%)	Other public entities (%)
Size						
Large	34.1	11.7	24.3	10.8	17.4	1.7
Medium-large	20.3	9.0	36.2	15.3	15.0	4.2
Medium	25.7	11.0	29.6	12.0	20.0	1.7
Medium-small	26.5	9.2	32.6	11.9	17.9	1.9
Small	11.5	12.6	41.4	8.5	24.7	1.3
Total	**31.5**	**11.3**	**26.4**	**11.4**	**17.4**	**2.0**
Geographic distribution						
Northwest	37.6	17.3	20.5	11.2	12.5	0.9
Northeast	29.3	5.1	31.1	12.0	20.9	1.7
Central	22.9	5.5	31.7	8.3	25.6	6.0
South and islands	11.3	15.1	38.6	21.4	13.0	0.6
Total	**31.5**	**11.3**	**26.4**	**11.4**	**17.4**	**2.0**

to individuals or organizations (e.g., associations, museums, local authorities, religious institutions), which in turn play a "brokering" role between the bank foundation and the territory.

In this way, a principle of horizontal subsidiarity is realized (Article 118, paragraph 4, of the Italian Constitution), in which bank foundations support the work of other organizations that in turn foster the cultural, social, and economic growth of the territory.

As Table 2.14 shows, the beneficiaries of grants received are both public entities (e.g., local authorities, schools, universities) and private nonprofit organizations (e.g., associations, foundations, religious institutions). It follows that Italian bank foundations are nonprofit institutions required to finance other nonprofit entities.

As Table 2.14 shows, the private sector received the largest part of the sums paid (69.2 % in 2012). Foundations (not those of banking origins) and associations were the main beneficiaries in 2012 and received, respectively, 31.5 % and 11.3 % of the disbursed amounts. The foundations were financed especially by large bank foundations concentrated in the northwest region of the country, which created some of the main instrumental foundations operating in Italy. Disbursements paid to associations were weighted equally for both large and small bank foundations.

The public sector received the remaining 30.8 % of disbursements. The nonterritorial public entities (e.g., schools, universities, local health organizations) and local authorities (e.g., municipalities, provinces) are the privileged partners of the bank foundations. In 2012, they absorbed, respectively, 11.4 % and 17.4 % of the sums paid.

References

ACRI (2013) Diciottesimo rapporto sulle fondazioni di origine bancaria. Rome
Alberti GB (2002) La determinazione dei risultati nelle fondazioni bancarie. Assetti istituzionali e modelli di bilancio. RIREA, Rome
Anheier HK (2001) Foundations in Europe: a comparative perspective. In: Schülter A, Then V, Walkenhorst P (eds) Foundations in Europe: society, management and law. Directory of Social Change, London, pp 35–81
Anheier HK (2005) Nonprofit organizations: theory, management, policy. Routledge, London/New York
Anheier HK, Leat D (2002) From charity to creativity: philanthropic foundations in the 21st century. COMEDIA in association with the Joseph Rowntree Reform Trust, London
Basile M (2003) Le persone giuridiche. Trattato di Diritto Privato. Giuffrè, Milan
Beyer H (1999) Toward an entrepreneurial approach to foundation management. In: Anheier HK, Toepler S (eds) Private funds and public purpose: philanthropic foundations in international perspectives. Plenum, New York, pp 155–162
Boesso G, Cerbioni F, Menini A, Parbonetti A (2011) Governo e prestazioni nelle fondazioni di origine bancaria. Il Risparmio 1:5–34
Bruni G (1999) L'azienda come sistema convertitore di valori economici in valori culturali. Il peculiare ruolo delle fondazioni comunitarie. RIREA 1:2–16
Bulmer M (1999) The history if foundations in the United Kingdom and the United States: philanthropic foundations in industrial society. In: Anheier HK, Toepler S (eds) Private funds and public purpose: philanthropic foundations in international perspectives. Plenum, New York, pp 27–53
Cioccarelli G, Previtali P (2002) Le Fondazioni ex bancarie. Orientamento strategico, assetto organizzativo e competenze manageriali. Giuffrè, Milan
Danzi L, Demarie M (2003) Fondazioni, una specie in via di estensione. Il Ponte 59(5):139–156
Emmanuele EFM (2004) Evoluzione e vicende delle fondazioni di origine bancaria. Edizioni Scientifiche Italiane, Turin
European Foundation Centre (2003) Typology of foundations in Europe. Brussels
European Foundation Centre (2005) Foundation facts & figures across the EU – associating private wealth for public benefit. Brussels
Karl B, Katz S (1987) Foundations and the ruling class. Daedalus 116(1):1–40
Leardini C (2005) L'amministrazione della fondazione bancaria. Cedam, Padua
Leardini C, Rossi G (eds) (2010) Fondazioni bancarie, arte e cultura Ruolo, risultati e prospettive alla luce di un'analisi territoriale. Franco Angeli, Milan
Leat D (1999) British foundations: the organization and management of grant-making. In: Anheier HH, Toepler S (eds) Private funds and public purpose. Philanthropic foundations in international perspectives. Plenum, New York, pp 121–140
McCarthy KD (1989) The gospel of wealth: American giving in theory and practice. In: Magat R (ed) Philanthropic giving: studies in varieties and goals. Oxford University Press, New York/Oxford
Merusi F (2002) Dalla banca pubblica alla fondazione privata. In: Studi in onore di Umberto Pototschnig, vol 1. Giuffrè, Milan
Salamon LM, Anheier HK (eds) (1997) Defining the nonprofit sector: a cross-national analysis. Manchester University Press, Manchester
Salamon L, Voytek K (1989) Managing foundation assets. The Foundation Centre, New York
Tieghi M (1995) Le fondazioni: obiettivi finalizzanti, sistema informativo e bilancio di esercizio. Clueb, Bologna
Tieghi M (2002) Le fondazioni bancarie. Riforma o controriforma? Egea, Milan
Zagrebelsky G (2009) Fondazioni di origine bancaria e democrazia partecipativa. Il Risparmio 3:25–44
Zamagni S (2007) Le Fondazioni di origine bancaria, motore di progresso civile. Il Risparmio 2:47–61

Chapter 3
Governance Roles and Responsibilities

3.1 Participants, Roles, and Responsibilities

The definition of the roles and the responsibilities of the different participants in a bank foundation and the underlying rules of decision making facilitate good governance.

Although Italian bank foundations are private legal entities with statutory and management autonomy, their legal origin affects their basic architecture and sets some constraints that do not necessarily apply to other foundations and nonprofit organizations.

The law regulates, in general terms, the purpose and mode of operation of bank foundations in the following ways:

- They must engage solely in social-oriented and economic development undertakings.
- They must manage their assets in a careful way, so that they maintain their value and produce an adequate return on investment.

Moreover, the law establishes the governance structure, focusing on the different roles and responsibilities of the two boards. This is a strong point of discontinuity compared with the governance of the other nonprofit organizations (see Miller-Millesen 2003).

The participants, roles, and responsibilities of the boards and the qualification of board members are defined under the law. The statutes have the task of regulating in greater detail the organizational structure of the bank foundations in accordance with the general principles established by law. The autonomy accorded to bank foundations therefore should be understood as the ability to define their own choices and rules within the overall limits dictated by the legislative system (ACRI 2012).

Article 4 of Legislative Decree no. 153/1999 provides for separate collective bodies for direction, administration, and control. It follows a "functional separation"—that is, a clear distinction among bodies that carry out different

C. Leardini et al., *Board Governance in Bank Foundations*, Contributions to Management Science, DOI 10.1007/978-3-642-41306-3_3,

functions. As a consequence, it also dictates a "personal separation"—that is, an incompatibility among positions. With the exception of the bank foundation president, a person cannot be a member of two boards at the same time.

The separation between functions is concomitant with a separation of responsibilities within the foundation. The different functions of the boards lead to different sets of responsibilities.

However, the bank foundation as a whole remains responsible toward its stakeholders. A foundation is like a living organism in which different organs operate with their own well-defined function. At the same time, and also like a living organism, the foundation is an entity fully responsible as a whole to third parties for its functioning.

The functional separation not only operates at the level of governance and macro structure but also represents the guiding principle that should inform any further organizational articulation of foundations (e.g., scientific committees, technical units of evaluation). It means that the tasks of the various boards should always be distributed following a clear distinction among functions and powers of direction, administration, and control.

Article 4, Paragraph 1, of Legislative Decree no. 153/1999—Bodies
The statutes, in defining the organizational structure of the foundations, shall comply with the following principles:

a. Provision of separate bodies for direction, administration, and control;
b. Attribution to the policy-making body of competences regarding the determination of programs, priorities, and objectives of the foundation and the verification of the results achieved, providing that the body acts in relation to:
    i. Approval and amendment of the statutes and internal regulations,
    ii. Appointment and dismissal of the administrative and control body members and determination of their payments,
    iii. Exercise of the liability action against the members of the administrative and control bodies,
    iv. Approval of the annual financial statements,
    v. Definition of the main guidelines of asset management and investment policy,
    vi. Transformation and merger;
c. Provision, within the policy-making body, for an adequate and qualified representation of the territory with particular reference to local authorities and for the presence of components with professionalism, competence, and experience in the areas where the foundation activity is directed, so that they can effectively contribute to the pursuance of institutional goals. The number of components has to be suited to ensuring the effective exercise of their respective duties and the procedures for designating and

(continued)

(continued)

appointing them should enable a balanced representation of the parties involved in the body formation;

d. Provision that foundations having associative origins may consider, in the exercise of their statutory autonomy, the maintenance of an assembly of the original associates and regulate its composition without conflicting with the competences of the policy-making body. The assembly may be assigned by statute the power to appoint a nonmajority portion of the policy-making body, in accordance with the provisions of letter c. In this case, the components nominated for designation of the assembly together with those appointed by co-optation, pursuant to paragraph 6, cannot exceed half of the total members of the policy-making body;
e. Assignment to the administrative body of the management of the foundation, as well as of proposal functions under the programs, priorities, and objectives set by the policy-making body;
f. Provision, within the governing bodies of foundations whose activities are addressed in specific regions by the respective statutes, of a representation of at least fifty per cent of people residing for at least three years in the same territories;
g. Identification for the members who perform direction, administration, and control functions of professionalism and integrity requirements, of cases of incompatibility referring also to the position of general manager in the spin-off bank or to external mandates or public office, and of causes that entail the temporary suspension from office or forfeiture, in order to avoid conflicts of interest and to ensure the independence in their respective duties and transparency of decisions;
h. Obligation of the foundation board members to give immediate notice of the grounds for revocation or suspension and the reasons for incompatibilities that affect them;
i. Expectation that members of the boards shall be appointed for delimited periods of time and can be confirmed only once;

The basic governance of Italian bank foundations is influenced in part by the original savings banks' characteristics. Some of them had institutional origins and were founded by local community entities. Others had associative origins and were the result of a private citizen's capital.

Therefore, the mandatory minimum model of governance of bank foundations includes the following (see Fig. 3.1):

- An assembly of the original associates (only for bank foundations having associative origins),
- A Board of Trustees,
- A Board of Directors, and
- An Audit Committee.

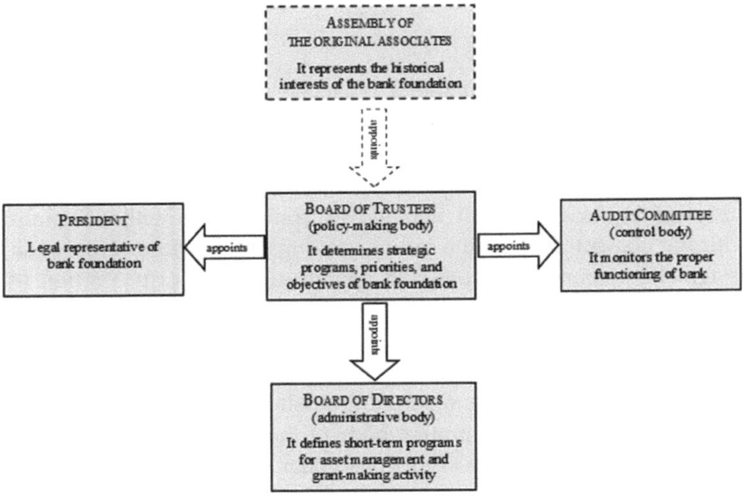

Fig. 3.1 Participants, roles, and responsibilities

With the exception of the assembly of the original associates, all the other government bodies are required. The governance is completed by the figure of the president, who is the legal representative of the foundation. The president oversees the proper functioning of the foundation and supervises the actions of the boards. In cases of dire necessity or urgency, the president may make decisions that are usually the provenance of the boards.

The principle of functional separation requires the presence of different boards within bank foundations. These boards have different roles that complement and complete the other board's functions and efforts.

The Board of Trustees is the policy-making body. It is in charge of strategic planning and has the duty of determining priorities, objectives, and multiannual programs, for both asset management and grant-making activities. It has the power to allocate for the long term the funds resulting from asset management to the grant-making activity, identifying the most relevant sectors in which the assets should be used.

The Board of Directors is in charge of translating the strategic plans set up by the Board of Trustees into short-term programs for the next year, for both asset management and the grant-making activity. Such programs must then be transmitted to management for implementation.

Finally, the Audit Committee is the control body and has the task of monitoring the proper functioning of the foundation.

The personal and functional separation between the bodies within a bank foundation creates a dialectic based on the distinction of roles, tasks, and responsibilities (Ristuccia 2007). It is therefore important that every organ has both a high level of professionalism in asset management and in the social field to allow for decisions of direction, management, and control, consistent with social and economic development objectives assigned to the bank foundations.

In this regard, the Board of Trustees and the Board of Directors may be supported by study commissions and committees of scientific and technical evaluation, both temporary and permanent, that have an advisory capacity regarding general or specific areas of intervention.

While leaving the composition of the governing bodies to statutory freedom, the law requires that the selection of members be carried out, taking into account the concrete strategic and operational needs of the foundation.

3.2 The Assembly of the Original Associates

The assembly of the original associates is a body often present in bank foundations with associative origins.

Some foundations have institutional origin (original savings banks were founded by local community entities), while others have associative origin (original savings banks were anonymous societies with capital contributed by private citizens). The only difference between the two is that the foundations with associative origin still hold assemblies of the original associates.

The only task that the law (Article 4 of Legislative Decree no. 153/1999) gives to the assembly is the possibility of designating a nonmajority portion of the Board of Trustees. Additional tasks may be established by the statutes, with the understanding that, in line with the principle of functional separation, the assembly cannot under any circumstances carry out the tasks entrusted to other bodies or interfere with them.

In general, the most common additional task of the assembly is to give voice and continuity to the original historical interests of the foundation. In this capacity, the assembly has functions similar to those typical of the colleges of arbitrators—namely, guaranteeing the observance of the foundation's code of ethics, protecting the interests of the recipients of interventions, and so forth.

The assembly may be called on to express its opinions, sometimes mandatory but nonbinding, about the multiannual programs prepared by the policy-making body, the internal regulations, and extraordinary transactions (e.g., mergers, transformations). Moreover, it can prepare documents that contribute to the proper accomplishment of the foundation's purposes and promote institutional proposals of intervention in the allowed sectors of activity.

The Assembly of the Original Associates Under the Statutes: Some Examples

Fondazione CR Perugia **– Article 7**

1. The associates represent the historical continuity of the Foundation with the original organization.

Ente Cassa di Risparmio di Firenze **– Article 10**

(continued)

(continued)

The assembly of the original associates is the body that represents the original continuity of the Institution, the associative values, and civil peculiarities inherited from a significant past, giving voice and continuity to the historical representation of the interests of the Organization. The assembly plays a role of witness and moral control, to better ensure the compliance with the statutory values and the consistency and transparency of the Organization.

***Fondazione Roma* – Article 9**

1. The assembly of the original associates represents the historical and legal continuity of the original function of the Foundation. It plays a role of general supervision of compliance with the provisions of the statute and the achievement of institutional goals.

***Fondazione CR Bolzano* – Article 16**

Without prejudice to the competence of the policy-making body, the assembly of original associates represents the historical interests of the Foundation, in the social and territorial context in which it operates.
Through the deliberation of proposals and petitions addressed to the organs, it promotes initiatives for the protection of the interests of the interventions' recipients and ensures adherence to the Foundation's code of ethics, expressing opinions and assessments on a proposal from the members.

3.3 The Board of Trustees

Within nonprofit organizations, the policy-making body is the body that should govern the institution. According to Ingram (2009), the policy-making body has four main objectives and responsibilities: legal and fiduciary, oversight, fundraising, and representation of constituencies and viewpoints. For this reason, the body has to:

- Determine the mission and purposes of the organization.
- Select the administrative body, support and evaluate it.
- Ensure effective planning and monitor and strengthen programs.
- Ensure adequate financial resources, protect assets, and provide financial oversight, as well as build a competent board ensuring legal and ethical integrity.
- Enhance the organization's public standing.

These considerations are applicable to nonprofit organizations in general, but they also apply to bank foundations.

Under a variety of names, the statutes identify the board that represents the policy-making body imposed by law, such as the "General Council," "Central Board of Charities," and "Board of Trustees" (herein, the term "Board of Trustees" is used because it is the most common).

The basic function of this body, however, does not change: It is the decision-making centre of the foundation, called to make choices that are fundamental to the institution. By law, the Board of Trustees is in charge of strategic planning and control, with the duty of determining the long-term programs, priorities, and objectives of the foundation, as well as verifying the results achieved.

The Board of Trustees: General Functions

Fondazione CR Verona Vicenza Belluno e Ancona – Article 11

1. The Board of Trustees is responsible for the pursuing of the Foundation's aims. It directs the activities of the foundation and verifies the results achieved.
2. The Board of Trustees:

    a. Determines the objectives of the Foundation, its priorities, and operational guidelines. In particular, it determines the programs, including long-term pro-grams, taking into account the peculiarities and the needs of the territory, identifying the sectors, among those allowed by law, in which to allocate from time to time the available funds;

    [. . .]

    d. Defines the general guidelines for asset management, investment policy and shareholdings.

Ente Cassa di Risparmio di Firenze – Article 12

The Board of Trustees is responsible for approving the general programs of the Institution and for the periodic verification of the achievement of the objectives, the priorities, and the quality of results.

The Board of Trustees:

a. Determines priorities and objectives of the Foundation with programmatic method and a multiyear approach and verifies the results achieved;
b. Indicates to the Board of Directors the measures it considers appropriate to adopt for the better attainment of the goals of the Foundation and for the fulfilment of its activities;
c. Monitors the functioning of the Foundation to ensure the pursuit of institutional goals and to defend the value of the net asset.

The Board of Trustees is the head of internal governance system. The law and the statutes confer to it numerous specific tasks and powers through which to implement the function of direction:

- It can define the general guidelines of the foundation's activity through the provision of multiannual planning document.
- It can approve and amend the statutes and the internal regulations.
- It can appoint and dismiss the members of the administrative and control bodies, determine their compensation, and exercise on them the liability action.
- It can approve the annual financial statements.
- It can define the main guidelines of asset management and investment policy.
- It can decide on extraordinary transactions (mergers and transformation).

To perform the strategic function that has been assigned to it and determine long-term programs, priorities, and objectives of the foundation in an effective way, the Board of Trustees must have a thorough knowledge of the needs to be met within the territory. In addition, it must be able to establish the priority of those needs. The needs to be satisfied are many; the financial resources available for the grant-making activity are scarce. It is therefore necessary to select which needs are to be met first. Finally, the Board of Trustees must be able to identify a set of guidelines for the realization of socially oriented and economic development projects and to generate the funds to achieve them through careful planning of asset management.

For these reasons, it is important that the members of the Board of Trustees have a high degree of professionalism and be representative of the foundation's stakeholders and their needs. The law merely states that this board must ensure an adequate and qualified representation of the territory (especially local authorities, such as municipalities, provinces, and regions) and comprise professional and experienced people who can contribute substantially to the achievement of institutional goals. The law then relies on the statutes of each foundation to carry out the task of regulating in detail the issue of the composition and the professionalism of the board.

The statute therefore must determine:

- The number of members to compose the Board of Trustees;
- The minimum requirements that they must meet;
- Who within the territory (e.g., local authorities, various associations, religious institutions) can nominate them;
- The procedure of nominating and appointing; and
- The term of office.

Because the foundation must operate in the exclusive interest of the territory, it is important that the members of the board are able to identify (in terms of a multiannual perspective) a map of the needs to be met, taking into account the reality that they vary in type, intensity, and priorities over time.

Of course, the provisions of the law and the statute regarding the composition of the Board of Trustees alone are not enough to ensure that the foundation faithfully pursues through its own choices in the general interests of the territory. It is a problem that is related not only to ethical behaviour but also, and more immediately, to the professionalism of the members of the decision-making body.

Beyond the composition, the statute must also identify the skills deemed most appropriate to effectively carry out the direction function. In general, members of the Board of Trustees must possess a set of leadership competences (Harrison and Murray 2012) that may increase the effectiveness of the bank foundation's activity. More specifically, the board must have the ability to understand complexity in the environment, identify a broad vision of the organization, identify the strategic priorities, acquire funds for the organization, develop strategic alliances in the community, and build trusting and supportive relationships with others.

These general leadership abilities should be completed by a set of professional qualifications and experiences both in asset management and in social realms, which lend themselves to the specific activity of the bank foundations. In particular, members with finance experience are essential for the asset management function and to ensure that return on investment is adequate to meet the requirements of the grant-making activity.

There is an additional factor that influences the effectiveness of the Board of Trustees' activity: its operation. Determining *how* the decision-making power is exercised within the board is of fundamental importance for assessing whether the foundation has the preconditions to operate in the interest of the territory as a whole. There is the risk that the main decisions pertaining to objectives, priorities, and programs are not derived and agreed on by the body as a whole but rather only by a select few of its members who take into account the needs of only particular categories of stakeholders. When personal motivations prevail in the strategic management choices, it creates a pathological situation because the foundation is not able to achieve the objectives that have been assigned to it.

One of the main operating mechanisms intended to ensure that the Board of Trustees makes decisions in the overall interest of the territory and not on behalf of specific groups of stakeholders is represented by the deliberative quorum. The *quorum* is the minimum number of members necessary to validate the board's meeting. In general, the statutes require the presence of at least a majority of the members in charge. The deliberative quorum indicates the minimum number of votes required for approval of the board's decisions. The statutes generally require that resolutions be passed by a majority of those present. However, it can require a more stringent quorum for resolutions pertaining to extraordinary acts, such as amendment of the statutes or regulations, transformations, mergers, dissolution of the foundation, and liability action.

3.4 The Board of Directors

In Italian bank foundations, the Board of Directors is appointed by the Board of Trustees and is responsible for meeting mandates and achieving set missions, goals, and strategies (Bryson 2011). Its task is to translate the multiannual strategic plans draw by the Board of Trustees into short-term programs for the next year.

The Board of Directors: General Functions

Fondazione Roma **– Article 25**

1. The Board of Directors has all the powers of ordinary and extraordinary administration, except those reserved to the Board of Trustees by law and by this statute.

Fondazione CR Verona Vicenza Belluno e Ancona **– Article 16**

1. The Board of Directors is the body responsible for the management of the Foundation within the objectives and programs established by the Board of Trustees. It carries out all activities that are necessary for the pursuit of the same, as well as activities of proposal to the Board of Trustees.

Fondazione CR Parma e Busseto **– Article 20**

1. The Board of Directors has all the powers of ordinary and extraordinary administration of the Foundation, except those expressly reserved for another organ of the Foundation by law or this statute. It exercises a proposal power to the Board of Trustees with regard to matters pertaining to the activities of the Foundation under the programs, priorities, and objectives set by the Board of Trustees, the establishment of instrumental enterprises as well as the definition of the programs of the foundation.

The relationship between the Board of Trustees and the Board of Directors can be understood as an agency relationship. The former delegates to the latter the duty to operationalize through annual plans the multiannual strategies defined for the long-term period, while the actual implementation and executive function is delegated to management. The Board of Trustees exercises the power of appointment and removal of directors, establishes guidelines for their actions, determines their compensation, verifies the results achieved, and enforces the liability action. The Board of Directors then acts on behalf of the Board of Trustees.

By law, the Board of Directors has all the powers of ordinary and extraordinary administration that are not under the responsibility of other organs on the basis of the principle of functional separation. In particular, it must:

- Prepare the annual planning document.

- Prepare the financial statements and the management report (Leardini and Rossi 2007).
- Implement the programs defined by the Board of Trustees through the multiannual planning document. In particular, the Board of Directors identifies and selects specific activities and interventions that are suitable to meet the needs of the territory identified as relevant by the Board of Trustees.
- Propose activities to the Board of Trustees related to the programs it has specified. The Board of Directors is therefore called on to support the policy-making body, but its role in the matter of strategic planning must be correctly identified. The Board of Directors, in effect, can only play an impulsive role because it lacks a long-term perspective (Cioccarelli and Previtali 2002). If this were not the case, the Board of Trustees would be reduced to a simple constituency or body in charge with the election of the Board of Directors. In this case, it would become a sort of honorary committee with a purely advisory function and no real authority over decisions. This could severely vitiate the direction–administration–control circuit intended by the law (Ristuccia 2007).
- Deliberate projects and disbursements consistent with the guidelines established in the multiannual planning document prepared by the Board of Trustees. In operational terms, this activity consists of two key moments: (1) the evaluation of the projects proposed by third parties (project content, means of implementation, reliability of the recipients in completing the project for which the funds are disbursed) to verify that they are in line with foundation's objectives, priorities, and programs and (2) the issue of the resolution, which identifies for each intervention the beneficiary and the amounts to be paid. A resolution establishes a real commitment for the foundation to finance the implementation of the project that the Board of Directors has approved. The priority levels identified by the Board of Trustees in the multiannual planning document should affect the timing of resolutions: The more urgent an intervention is, the faster the activity of the Board of Directors should be.
- Manage the foundation's assets in accordance with the criteria set by the Board of Trustees or entrust their management to outside institutional investors to ensure an adequate return on investment.
- Establish internal regulations governing the operation of the various offices and attend to organizational and personnel matters.

Similar to the Board of Trustees, to carry out these tasks effectively, the Board of Directors must be equipped with a high and diversified sense of professionalism pertaining both to asset management and to grant-making activity. In particular, the members of the Board of Directors must have appropriate expertise in matters pertaining to the specific areas of intervention in which the foundation operates and to financial sectors and securities. They must also have adequate operational experience in a professional, business, or academic setting or experience in direction and administrative functions in the public or private sector.

There must also be a proper coordination with the Board of Trustees to ensure that its guidelines are translated into management operations. This coordination should be ensured by the agency relationship that binds the two bodies. However, the lack of objective measurement pertaining to the operating results, because there is no monetary payment in return for the services provided through grant-making activities, undermines the main instrument on which control over directors' work is typically based (Alberti 2002). Because market mechanisms are ineffective for bank foundations, there is a need to limit the discretion of the Board of Directors through appropriate control tools (Cioccarelli and Previtali 2002).

3.5 The Audit Committee

The Audit Committee is appointed by the Board of Trustees and generally consists of three members. It ensures the legitimacy and the proper work of the bank foundation. Therefore, it verifies that the foundation has achieved its objectives without contravening the provisions of the law and the statute.

With reference to the Audit Committee, the legislature did not set any specific rules, omitting any indication of the type of control that such a body should exercise. The law states only that the committee should be composed of people who have professional requirements for the statutory audit. In most cases, the provisions contained in the statutes are equally inadequate.

In addition to the duty of monitoring compliance with the law and the statute, the Audit Committee is responsible for monitoring the sense of respect for the principles of good administration; the adequacy of the organizational, administrative, and accounting procedures; and the operation of the bank foundation. For this reason, the committee participates (without voting rights) in the meetings of the Board of Trustees and the Board of Directors.

Control over the financial statements is generally entrusted to an external auditing company that works closely with the Audit Committee.

In addition to the requirements of integrity and professionalism provided by law for the exercise of the statutory audit, the members of the control body must possess skills consistent with the two basic activities carried out in bank foundations—asset management and grant-making activity—that they must monitor. Both activities require a different set of skills and carry a different set of risks.

3.6 Governance Principles Within the *Charter of the Foundations*

To ensure a minimum of uniformity in the matter of governance, in 2012, the Italian Association of Foundations of banking origin (ACRI) approved the *Charter of the Foundations*, a voluntary but binding code of conduct for all bank foundations (ACRI 2012). The document provides an example of self-regulation activity

(Gunningham and Rees 1997), inclusive of standards and rules of conduct set by an industry-level organization rather than a governmental apparatus, to complement state regulation, institutionalize good practices, and enhance legitimacy (Bies 2010).

The *Charter of the Foundations* emphasizes the importance of governance and draws up some reference guidelines common for all foundations. It is not a list of mandatory rules but rather a set of principles and criteria that each bank foundation can adopt in its statutory and/or regulatory requirements, operating procedures, and practices to inspire its own action.

The principles laid down in the *Charter of the Foundations* are as follows (ACRI 2012):

- Autonomy,
- Responsibility,
- Representativeness,
- Authority and competence of the boards,
- Independence of the boards,
- Transparency,
- Incompatibility and ineligibility,
- Authority and competence of appointments in subsidiaries and associates,
- Stability and continuity,
- Profitability, and
- Cooperation with other foundations.

3.6.1 Autonomy, Independence, and Cooperation

A first principle that should guide the governance of bank foundations, from its design, is autonomy. It is an essential character and necessary requirement for not only bank foundations but any organization in general (Azzini 1964; Bruni 1999; Ferrero 1967). Autonomy underlies the power of an organization to self-determine the set of rules to which it will submit (Wiberg 1998).

Considering the intrinsic nature of bank foundations, there is no doubt that there are deep connections among foundations, the territory, and the entities that operate within it. Bank foundations act in the exclusive interest of the local community, often in partnership with other agencies and organizations. The function of listening to the needs of the territory therefore is essential (ACRI 2012), and the cooperation with other organizations, especially among bank foundations, is promoted by the *Charter of the Foundations* as a principle to achieve shared goals.

However, bank foundations must make their own choices, free from interferences or external constraints that limit their autonomy. Autonomy is the ability to self-define the elements of the decision-making process, from the identification of the problem, to the selection of alternatives, and ultimately to the choices (Leardini 2012). It follows that bank foundations must define their strategy in full freedom and independence, and they must be able to identify independently the means of intervention that are most suitable to accomplish their statutory purposes.

Relationships with other organizations (public and private) in turn must be conducted on the basis of collaboration and cooperation, mutual respect, and autonomy for each partner's decision-making prerogatives.

Autonomy: Some Examples from the Statutes

***Fondazione CR Bolzano* – Article 34**

The members of the Board of Trustees act in full autonomy and independence. They do not represent those who have nominated them and carry out their duties without a binding mandate. They must act in the interest of the Foundation to achieve the purposes indicated in the statute.

***Ente Cassa di Risparmio di Firenze* – Article 4**

The Foundation takes initiative for its determination and autonomous choice and proceeds according to operational projects, with a coordinated set of actions aimed at achieving the objectives indicated through the multiannual planning.

***Fondazione CR Lucca* – Article 4**

Strategic guidelines, specific objectives to be pursued, priorities and lines of action, sectors, manner of action, and general criteria for disbursement are defined by the Board of Trustees, in order to ensure the efficient utilization of funds and the effectiveness of interventions, also with regard to the planned interventions by other agencies and institutions operating in the same geographical area.

Within bank foundations, the power to freely make choices is not a power of the organization in itself but rather a power of the governing bodies with direction and administrative functions. It follows that, to protect the autonomy and independence of the foundation and to avoid conflicts of interest, people who hold political office cannot participate in the governance bodies. The statutes identify the measures that are necessary to ensure that political offices and government of the foundation do not overlap (principle of incompatibility).

Consistent with the principle of functional separation, the offices within different boards are mutually incompatible, the only exception being the foundation's president, who can work as part of the Board of Trustees and the Board of Directors. If a member of a board takes a post in another organ of the foundation, this member shall then automatically be excluded from the first office.

This principle is designed to ensure the independence and transparency of the decisions made by the various organs.

3.6.2 Responsibility

Bank foundations play a key role in social and economic life, both as philanthropic institutions and as important institutional investors. Therefore the notion of responsibility—and along with it, accountability—is a central theme (Leardini and Rossi 2010).

Because bank foundations pursue social utility and promote economic development in the exclusive interest of the community (Article 4 of Legislative Decree no. 153/99), they are responsible to the community for their service. They are not, therefore, self-referential entities; on the contrary, they need to legitimize their very existence (Heydeman and Toepler 2006).

Bank foundations have the responsibility to meet the needs of the local community in an appropriate and prompt way. Specific responsibilities of the boards correspond to this overall responsibility of the foundation. These responsibilities account for the effectiveness and efficiency of their work.

Each board has different responsibilities in accordance with the principle of functional separation. The Board of Trustees is responsible for defining purposes, mandates, goals, issues, and strategies, whereas the Board of Directors is responsible for meeting mandates and achieving set missions, goals, and strategies (Bryson 2011).

> ***Fondazione CR Verona Vicenza Belluno e Ancona***
> **Article 11** – The Board of Trustees is the body responsible for the pursuit of the institutional goals of the Foundation. It directs the activities of the Foundation and verifies the results.
> **Article 16** – The Board of Directors is the body responsible for the management of the Foundation within the objectives and programs established by the Board of Trustees. It carries out all activities that are necessary for the pursuit of the same, as well as proposal activities to the Board of Trustees.

The responsibility-taking process of the governing bodies is supported by internal accountability (Leardini and Rossi 2007). In particular, internal accountability is the process of checking whether the funds used produced a result in line with the mission and strategic objectives of the foundation (Ebrahim 2003).

Responsibility goes hand in hand with accountability. It is necessary not only to become aware of responsibilities through internal accountability but also to demonstrate compliance with the commitments through external accountability.

External accountability shows the foundation's stakeholders how funds have been used. This form of accountability represents a means of communication, as well as a way to be accountable to those who are aligned with but are external to the organization (Cornwall et al. 2000). For this reason, accountability for bank foundations is not just a duty required by law; it also constitutes a central focus of their administration through which they come to know and make known the results of their operations in the field (Braverman 2003).

Common to all bank foundations, the primary documents used to provide external accountability are financial statements and management reports, including the mission report (Moggi and others 2012). These documents reveal the strategies and choices that bank foundations have made and measure the results achieved (Leardini and Rossi 2007).

The financial statement specifies the financial and economic results of any activities (Legislative Decree no. 153/1999, Article 9, paragraph 5, a). This set of documents derives from accounting reviews (e.g., balance sheet, income statement, notes) and highlights the foundation's income and capital, offering a general overview of its financial situation (Tieghi 2002). However, financial statements cannot offer detailed information about the specific areas in which the foundation has chosen to operate. For this reason, they are not enough to prove that the boards of the foundation have been operating in the exclusive interest of the territory.

Such information instead appears in the management report and, in particular, in the mission report. The mission report attempts to describe, in a less technical way that is accessible and understandable to stakeholders, the activities carried out in the different intervention areas (Rusconi 2005). For each area, the mission report details the social objectives pursued, the activities carried out, and the results obtained.

So that the external accountability mechanism can effectively support the responsibility-taking process, both the financial statement and the mission report must include some common characteristics (Rossi 2009). In particular, the reports must be transparent, reliable, and complete, as well as accessible to all stakeholders. They also must describe the reality without defections or distortions. If they meet these standards, external accountability becomes a powerful tool for communicating with stakeholders and legitimating foundation activity.

3.6.3 *Representativeness and Independence of the Boards*

To operate effectively in favor of the territory, the governing bodies of the bank foundations must have a thorough knowledge of the needs to be met through the grant-making activity. They must also know their degree of urgency to determine what needs to meet first with the limited funds that are available.

Thus, it is important that the members of the governing boards are representative of the community in which the foundation is active. Only in this way will they be able to capture and convey the needs of the territory. This matter is particularly tied to the composition of the Board of Trustees.

According to the law (Article 4, paragraph 1, letter c. of Legislative Decree no. 153/1999), the board must ensure an adequate representation of the territory. For this reason, the statutes identify the institutions, local authorities, and other bodies, organizations, or associations granted the power to appoint members of the board.

It is important to emphasize, however, that the members of the Board of Trustees do not represent the organizations that appointed them (Zagrebelsky 2009). They have no binding mandate and are free to act in total and absolute independence of these organizations. The mechanism of the designation must therefore be understood as a tool to bring together into a single entity (the Board of Trustees) experiences, skills, and different professional capacities, with the aim of contributing to the attainment of the objectives assigned to the foundation.

The law is clear on this point: Article 4, paragraph 2, of Legislative Decree no. 153/1999 states that the members of the Board of Trustees neither represent the parties that appointed them nor respond to them. The members of the boards therefore act in the interests of foundations, consistent with the principle of autonomy recognized in these institutions.

Focus: The Sentence no. 301/2003 of the Constitutional Court
At the end of a long debate, the Constitutional Court judgment no. 301/2003 established that the Board of Trustees members are representative of the territory, but they do not represent the institutions which have nominated them.
In particular, the Court highlighted that the term representation is "used by the legislator (also within the Legislative Decree no. 153/1999) in order to indicate the relationship between the entities recalled by the norm and the persons they designated as members of the Board of Trustees. These institutions, in fact, have a power of appointment for members of the Board of Trustees, that runs out with its use, and that does not involve any binding mandate against those appointed, which act, and should act, in complete and total independence from the institution which appointed them."

In the matter of representation, the *Charter of the Foundations* also specifies that the composition of the governing bodies must ensure an adequate representation of gender. This statement reflects an important reform in Italian corporate law realized through the Golfo-Mosca Law no. 120/2011, which introduced gender quotas in the composition of the administrative and control boards of listed companies and state-owned companies.

More specifically, the law dictates that a minimum quota of the less representative gender serve on both the Board of Directors and the Audit Committee—specifically, at least one-fifth at the time of the first renewal of the organs and at least one-third during the second and third renewal (Rossi 2013).

Bank foundations are not among the organizations subject to this legal obligation. However, they draw on these principles on a voluntary basis to promote gender diversity as a source of variety of skills, diversity of perspective, and difference of viewpoints among the members of the board (Burke 1997; Dunn 2012).

3.6.4 Authority and Competence of the Boards and Transparency

The activities that governing bodies perform require skills, experience, and professionalism in asset management and grant-making activity. These skills vary with the function of the body (i.e., direction, management, or control), but they are all equally functional to the effective pursuit of the institutional goals of the foundation.

The statute thus is called on to establish the necessary requirements of authority and professionalism, the educational qualifications or academic competences, and experiences that are appropriate to the tasks to be performed. When possible, this duty can also be delegated to specific internal regulations.

The principle stated by the *Charter of the Foundations* underlines what has already been established by the law—namely, that members of the governing bodies have adequate professional qualifications and integrity, understood as the ethical suitability to enact the roles of government within a nonprofit organization.

Integrity Requirements in the Statutes

***Fondazione Cassa di Risparmio di Parma e Busseto* – Article 8**

1. The members of the Foundation's governing bodies and the general secretary shall be chosen among persons of full civil capacity and unquestioned probity.
2. They cannot be designated or appointed in the Foundation's boards nor assume the position of general secretary or, if appointed, shall be removed from office:

    a. Those who find themselves in one of the conditions laid down by art. 2382 of the Civil Code or those who have held high offices in the administration or management of companies subject to bankruptcy, receivership, compulsory liquidation, or other insolvency proceedings or similar procedures;
    b. Those who have been subjected to precautionary measures imposed by the court under the law of 27 December 1956 no. 1423 or 31 May 1965 no. 575, and subsequent amendments and additions, the effects of rehabilitation excepted;
    c. Those who have been convicted by a judgment even if not definitive, the effects of rehabilitation excluded:

        i. to imprisonment for an offense under the rules governing the banking, financial, brokerage, and insurance activity and the rules governing markets, securities, and payment instruments;

(continued)

(continued)

ii. to imprisonment for one of the crimes provided for in Title XI of Book V of the Civil Code and Royal Decree of 16 March 1942 no. 267;
iii. to imprisonment for a period not less than one year for crimes against the public administration, public faith, heritage, public order, and public economy as well as for any other intentional crime;

d. Those who were sentenced to one of the punishments mentioned in letter c with a judgment that assigns a penalty at the request of the parties, except in the case of extinction of the offense.

The presence of expertise can be connected to the constraint of responsibility. Because bank foundations pursue social utility and the promotion of economic development, their statutes must adjust the composition of the bodies so that they can acquire the skills necessary to decide and act in the interest of the territory.

The authority and competence of members of the Board of Trustees must be balanced with the requirement that the board is also representative of the territory. For this reason, the statutes should establish the requirements of professionalism in general and objective terms to avoid the foundation unduly limiting the power of appointment recognized to the organizations that represent the territory.

Professional Requirements of the Board of Trustees

***Fondazione cassa di risparmio di Cuneo* – Article 13**

The members of the Board of Trustees must possess expertise that is appropriate with the areas of intervention or that are functional to the Foundation's activities. They must have gained operational experiences in the professional, business, or academic field or must have covered executive or administration roles within public or private organizations.

***Fondazione Cassa di Risparmio di Padova e Rovigo* – Article 17**

The Foundation's President and the other members of the Board of Trustees must be chosen according to professionalism and expertise criteria that are suited to the purposes of the Foundation, including:

a. Persons who have adequate and qualified experiences in the areas of intervention under article 4 of the Statute, also gained through teaching and research;

(continued)

(continued)

b. Persons who have distinguished themselves for a particular commitment to the social, artistic, or cultural field;
c. Persons who have carried out administration, control, or management functions in public institutions or in companies of adequate size.

With regard to the Board of Directors, however, it may be appropriate that the statutes provide for specific selective-comparative procedures to identify the members who are better suited to carry out administrative duties within the foundation.

Professional Requirements of the Board of Directors

***Fondazione Cassa di Risparmio di Verona Vicenza Belluno e Ancona* – Article 14**

The members of the Board of Directors must possess an appropriate expertise in matters related to areas of intervention or activities that are functional for the Foundation or related to the financial sector. They must have gained a sufficient operating experience within a profession or in a business or academic field, or they must have held executive or administrative roles within public or private organizations.

***Compagnia di San Paolo* – Article 2**

The members of the Board of Directors must possess the requirements of integrity and professionalism provided in this Statute. Their appointment resolution shall comprise the method adopted for the choice and the existence of requirements of professionalism, experience, and expertise appropriate to the specific function to be performed.

The same law explicitly requires that the control body is made up of people who meet the requirements necessary to exercise the statutory audit. If the foundation deems additional requirements necessary, they should be expressed in statute.

The same principle of authority and expertise also applies to the members of the foundation's subsidiary or investee companies.

To promote the candidacy of any person in possession of the necessary requirements and to make transparent the mechanisms of selection, foundations must clarify the profiles of competences deemed most suitable to fill the positions. In addition, once the organs have been formed, they must identify appropriate ways to make public the profile of each member.

3.6.5 The Other Principles

The last two principles pertaining to governance complete the guidelines provided in the *Charter of the Foundations*.

The principle of stability and continuity has the purpose of ensuring the operational functionality of the bank foundation and avoiding situations of instability in the governance or discontinuity in the action of the foundation. This principle must be properly balanced with the seemingly opposite need to guarantee a regular replacement of board members. At present, this last need is realized by imposing a limited term on the offices and a limit to the number of mandates that each person can carry out.

To mitigate the two conflicting requirements, the *Charter of the Foundations* promotes a gradual renewal of the boards, to be pursued through mechanisms such as the partial replacement of their components, the time lag of the office's terms, and the different durations of the boards. In this way, rotation, stability, and functionality may proceed hand in hand.

Finally, the principle of profitability pertains to the proper use of funds. This principle is a general guideline for foundations that is instrumental for carrying out their institutional activity with continuity (Airoldi et al. 1994). It requires that foundations pursue the effectiveness and efficiency of their activity.

In relation to governance, the principle suggests that the remunerations paid to board members must be commensurate with the tasks performed, the responsibilities assumed, the foundation's size, and the amount of total operating expenses.

References

ACRI (2012) Diciassettesimo rapporto sulle fondazioni di origine bancaria. Rome

Airoldi G, Brunetti G, Coda V (1994) Economia aziendale. Il Mulino, Bologna

Alberti GB (2002) La determinazione dei risultati della gestione delle fon-dazioni bancarie. RIREA, Rome

Azzini L (1964) Autonomia e collaborazione tra le aziende. Giuffrè, Milan

Bies AL (2010) Evolution of nonprofit self-regulation in Europe. Nonprof Volunt Sec Q 39 (6):1057–1086

Braverman M (ed) (2003) Foundations and evaluation: contexts and practices for effective philanthropy. Jossey Bass, San Francisco

Bruni G (1999) L'azienda come sistema convertitore di valori economici in valori culturali. Il peculiare ruolo delle fondazioni comunitarie. RIREA 1:2–16

Bryson JM (2011) Strategic planning for public and nonprofit organizations, 4th edn. Jossey-Bass, San Francisco

Burke RJ (1997) Women on corporate boards of directors: a needed resource. J Bus Ethics 16:909–915

Cioccarelli G, Previtali P (2002) Le Fondazioni ex bancarie. Orientamento strategico, assetto organizzativo e competenze manageriali. Giuffrè, Milan

Cornwall A, Lucas H, Pasteur K (2000) Introduction: accountability through participation. IDS Bull 3(1):1–13

Dunn P (2012) Breaking the boardroom gender barrier: the human capital of female corporate directors. J Manag Gov 16:557–570
Ebrahim A (2003) Making sense of accountability. Nonprofit Manag Leadersh 14(2):191–212
Ferrero G (1967) Le determinazioni economico-quantitative d'azienda. Giuffrè, Milan
Gunningham N, Rees J (1997) Industry self-regulation. Law Policy 19(4):393–414
Harrison YD, Murray V (2012) Perspectives on the leadership of chairs of nonprofit organization boards of directors. A grounded theory mixed-method study. Nonprofit Manag Leadersh 22 (4):411–437
Heydeman S, Toepler S (2006) Foundations and the challenge of legitimacy in comparative perspective. In: Prewitt K, Dogan M, Heydeman S, Toepler S (eds) The legitimacy of philanthropic foundations. Russell Sage, New York, pp 150–174
Ingram RT (2009) Ten basic responsibilities of nonprofit boards. BoardSource, Washington, DC
Leardini C (2012) L'autonomia nelle decisioni aziendali. Giappichelli, Turin
Leardini C, Rossi G (2007) Aspetti critici del bilancio di esercizio delle Fondazioni di origine bancaria. RIREA, Rome
Leardini C, Rossi G (eds) (2010) Fondazioni bancarie, arte e cultura. Franco Angeli, Milan
Miller-Millesen JL (2003) Understanding the behavior of nonprofit boards of directors: a theory-based approach. Nonprof Volunt Sec Q 32(4):521–547
Moggi S, Leardini C, Rossi G, Cantele S (2012) The social reporting in Italian bank foundations. Paper presented at the 4th Italian conference on social and environmental accounting research, Levico Terme, 20–21 Sept 2012
Ristuccia S (2007) Le grandi fondazioni: una speciale responsabilità sociale. Il Risparmio 1:5–26
Rossi G (2009) La comunicazione aziendale. Franco Angeli, Milan
Rossi G (2013) Tempo di donne negli organi di governo delle società: la prospettiva economico-aziendale. In: Brollo M, Serafin S (eds) Donne, Politica e Istituzioni: il tempo delle donne. Forum, Udine, pp 183–190
Rusconi (2005) Il bilancio di missione delle Fondazioni: una proposta di rendicontazione sociale. ACRI, Rome
Tieghi M (2002) Le fondazioni bancarie. Riforma o controriforma? Egea, Milan
Wiberg M (1998) Political autonomy: ambiguities and clarifications. In: Suksi M (ed) Autonomy: applications and implications. Kluwer Law International, The Hague/Boston, pp 43–57
Zagrebelsky G (2009) Fondazioni di origine bancaria e democrazia partecipativa. Il Risparmio 3:25–44

Chapter 4
Composition of the Boards

4.1 Defining Composition for Good Governance

The composition of the boards plays a key role in bank foundations' governance.

The European Foundation Centre (2007) establishes in the Principle of Good Practice N.2 that "foundations have an identifiable decision-making body whose members and successors should be nominated in accordance with established principles and procedures, and act with the highest ethical standards."

Size, how members are chosen, the process of designation, the characteristics of the members, and gender diversity are all elements that contribute to good governance and thus need to be considered when appointing the Board of Trustees and the Board of Directors.

The number of members must be adequate to ensure the effective exercise of the duties assigned to the board and should be considered with respect to the size of the foundation, the local environment, and the areas of activity. However, there are no fixed minimum or maximum limitations; in each case, the bank foundation must consider its asset dimension and its field of activity in terms of the specific territory served and the sectors of interests. The number of members is fixed by the statutes, taking into account the aforementioned principle of adequacy.

The size of the boards changes in relation to the foundation size. As Table 4.1 shows, the mean number of the members increases with the size of the foundation, in accordance with the adequacy principle established by law. In this sense, on the one hand, too few members could limit the competences and the knowledge necessary for good governance; on the other hand, too many members could hinder the normal functioning of the boards.

Table 4.2 presents the mean of how many people are in charge in the two boards on a geographical basis. The data demonstrate a greater number of members in bank foundations in the northern region of Italy, likely the result of the high number of large bank foundations in this area. With this reasoning, it follows that there is a lower concentration of board members in bank foundations in the south and islands region.

C. Leardini et al., *Board Governance in Bank Foundations*, Contributions to Management Science, DOI 10.1007/978-3-642-41306-3_4,

Table 4.1 Mean number of the members on boards, by foundation size

Bank foundations size	N	Mean members of the Board of Trustees	Mean members of the Board of Directors
Small	18	14.3	6.0
Medium-small	17	17.1	6.6
Medium	18	19.5	7.0
Medium-large	17	20.4	7.0
Large	18	22.9	7.3
Total	**88**	**18.8**	**6.8**

Table 4.2 Mean number of the members on boards, by geographical area

Geographical area	N	Mean members Board of Trustees	Mean members Board of Directors
North	46	19.6	7.1
Central	35	18.0	6.6
South and islands	7	18.0	5.7
Total	**88**	**18.8**	**6.8**

In general, the composition of the Board of Trustees is conditioned by the particular nature of bank foundations, their origin, and their mission. Whereas in nonprofits, the board composition partially reflects the donation structure of the organization (Glaser 2003), in bank foundations, the Board of Trustees does not represent the stakeholders, but rather, in a more general sense, represents the territory in which the foundation is active.

In terms of composition of the Board of Trustees, the following elements must be considered:

- The number of members of the board,
- The people called to choose these members,
- The process of designation, and
- The term of office of the board members.

The statutes also define the rules for choosing who can nominate the board members and the procedure for nominating them. New members of the Board of Trustees are designated by different stakeholder groups, then appointed by the outgoing members of the board.

These statutes identify the institutions, bodies, organizations, and associations with the power to propose nominations. The choice is made based on the specific characteristics of the territory in which the foundation operates and may also include the criteria of rotation or shift work among several entities within the same type (e.g., local authorities).

The only constraint imposed by law is an adequate balance among the different actors involved in the formation of the organ, to be achieved through a balanced distribution of power.

The proposed nominations must be in the foundation's interest. It follows that the nominations are not binding for the foundation, which has the power to appoint the members of the Board of Trustees. This explains the widespread practice of not requiring the nomination of a single candidate but rather of a pool of names. In this sense, the foundation is able to choose among different candidates, taking into account the skills required for achieving its mission, objectives, and long-term strategies.

The law requires only that the members of the board form an adequate representation of the territory (especially with regard to local authorities) and are selected among people who can effectively contribute to the activities of the foundation with professionalism, competence, and experience. In this regard, Spear et al. (2009) note the difficulties of recruiting board members in nonprofit organizations who have sufficient skills and experience.

When the foundation operates exclusively in a particular territory, the law also requires that at least half the members are residents for at least 3 years in the same territory. The definition of the competences of the candidates is one of the most difficult criteria to meet (Young 2011).

With regard to the term of office, the members of the Board of Trustees hold office for a limited period and may be reappointed only once. Within this constraint, the statutes can determine the duration of the charge.

In the spirit of good governance, this period should be different from that of the administrative and control boards. In this way, it is easier to balance the need for a stable policy-making activity with that of ensuring a periodic renewal of skills and experiences of the board members.

This statute provision also applies to the Board of Directors. The law establishes that the statutes can determine the composition, the tasks, and the responsibilities of the administrative body. Composition policies for the Board of Directors also take into account the same rules as those fixed for the Board of Trustees, based on the adequacy principle. In line with the particular function of the Board of Directors, its composition must be useful for defining short-terms plans that are congruent with the foundation's mission.

The members of the Board of Directors are appointed by the Board of Trustees and include people who have the general requirement of honorability established by statute, in addition to certain professional requirements. In this regard, the statutes may provide an appropriate selection procedure to ensure that the expertise of the members of the board is adequate for accomplishing specific tasks.

Considering the importance of diversity within boards for achieving good governance (Bradshaw et al. 1996; Brown 2002), we analyzed the presence of women on boards of the 88 Italian bank foundations (see Table 4.3). As Brown (2002) emphasizes, it is important, both politically and operationally, for the organization to take into account diversity in the selection of boards members.

Consistent with the current situation in for-profit boards, the presence of women on the bank foundation boards is also limited. Only 12.85 % of the members of Boards of Trustees and 10.05 % of the Board of Directors are women. In the 88 bank foundations examined, there are three female presidents, and they reside only in the small foundations. The number of women on Boards of Trustees is higher than the mean (2.5) in the large (2.8), medium-large (3.3), and medium (2.8)

Table 4.3 Women on board in bank foundations, by foundation size

		President		Women on Boards of Trustees		Women on Board of Directors	
Bank foundations size	N	Men	Women	Mean	%	Mean	%
Large	18	18	0	2.8	12.35	0.6	7.63
Medium-large	17	17	0	3.3	16.14	0.9	12.61
Medium	18	18	0	2.8	13.39	0.6	7.94
Medium-small	17	17	0	1.8	10.00	0.6	8.85
Small	18	15	3	1.7	11.67	0.8	13.89
Total	**88**	**85**	**3**	**2.5**	**12.85**	**0.7**	**10.05**

bank foundations, while it is lower than the mean in medium-small (1.7) and small (1.7) foundations. On Boards of Directors, independent of the foundation size, female board members are rare.

With regard to gender distribution in the three Italian geographical areas (Table 4.4), it is important to consider why there is a higher mean number of female members on Boards of Trustees in the northern region of Italy (3.0) and a lower number in the south and islands (1.6). This increase can be linked to the different traditions of the local community called to choose these members. On Boards of Directors, however, the trend is different; there is no a direct link with the community because members are selected by the Board of Trustees.

4.2 Multistakeholder Governance

Nonprofit boards are often composed of a variety of members to reflect the numerous stakeholders' interests. This involves a complex structure of motivations and values (Ostrower and Stone 2006) summarized in a monolithic body (Jegers 2009).

Consistent with their specific historical origin, bank foundations have the mission to pursue the social utility of the territory. Therefore, good governance must mirror the territory. In this sense, the boards need to represent the various interests of the stakeholders.

As Donaldson and Preston (1995) emphasize, the organization requires different ways to be responsive to its stakeholders. One such way is a managerial approach, which considers stakeholder needs for establishing the organizational structure, general policies, and decision making.

Nonprofit organizations must draw a clear stakeholder map because they are private institutions called on to pursue a public purpose. This aspect is crucial in bank foundations, whose mission is to meet the needs of the local communities of the territory from which they originated. For this reason, mapping foundations' stakeholders is the starting point for strategic definition and, in general, for good governance.

Table 4.4 Women on board in bank foundations, by geographical area

		President		Women in Boards of Trustees		Women in Boards of Directors	
Geographical area	N	Men	Women	Mean	%	Mean	%
North	46	44	2	3.0	15.21	0.7	9.85
Central	35	34	1	2.0	10.30	0.7	10.34
South and islands	7	7	0	1.6	8.73	0.6	10.00
Total	**88**	**85**	**3**	**2.5**	**12.85**	**0.7**	**10.05**

Thus, understanding the needs of stakeholders allows the foundation to define strategies and objectives congruent with the core mission. To this end, Barrett (2001) presents three forms of community engagement:

- Participation of stakeholders in management and/or governance of the organization,
- Reporting to stakeholders on quality and effectiveness of service provision, and
- Reporting to donors and/or funders on what the organization's resources are used for and the effectiveness of the services provided.

Italian bank foundations typically embody the first of these forms, as this approach enables the foundation to most effectively take into account the heterogeneous interests of the territory.

4.2.1 *Who Chooses Members of the Board of Trustees?*

Because bank foundations have historical origins linked with the territory and the local community, they have a complex group of stakeholders (Fig. 4.1).

These groups of stakeholders are in some ways directly linked to the bank foundation's activity, yet in other ways, they must, by law, remain separated from the foundation to prevent conflicts of interest.

"Local stakeholders" include the broadest group of people who have an interest in the functioning of the foundation. This group essentially comprises the local community that is indirectly influenced by the activity of the foundation. The law enables these stakeholders to appoint the members who will serve on the Board of Trustees. These members, in turn, are called "governance stakeholders" and are chosen for their specific personal characteristics, such as knowledge of the foundation's field of action or their general professional credentials. They have the task of governing the foundation with respect to the various interests of the local community they represent.

The preceding categories of stakeholders should not be confused with "mission stakeholders," who are the people, group of people, or organizations benefiting directly from the bank foundation's grant-making activity. The law clearly emphasizes this point because it is important to prevent the risk of opportunistic behavior.

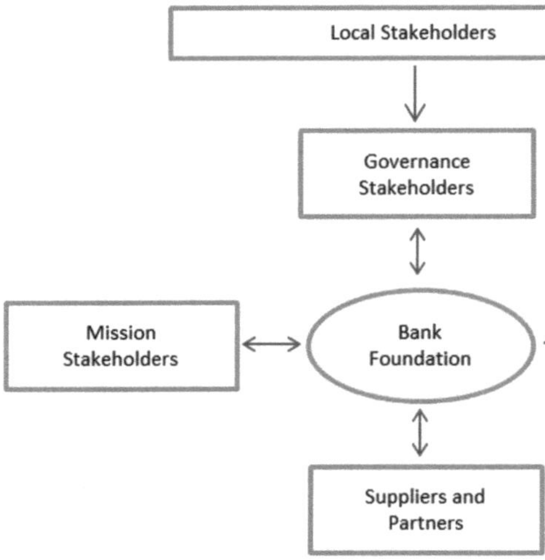

Fig. 4.1 Bank foundations' stakeholders

Mission stakeholders receive funds for supporting the foundation's activity in one or more of the sectors of interest. Included in this category are those who benefit directly from the initiative, such as a single person, the community, and future generations.

The "asset management stakeholders" also cannot be included in the bank foundation's board because they are responsible for managing the foundation's assets, and they cannot be both beneficiaries of the grant and responsible for strategic definition. In the Italian bank foundation context, these stakeholders are usually represented by banks or other financial institutions.

The last category of stakeholders is the "supplier and partner." This category includes the people or organizations that contribute to the daily activity of a bank foundation. This group comprises suppliers of goods and services the foundation uses to implement its activities. Also included in this category are people and organizations engaged in defining the community's needs, such as other nonprofit organizations belonging to a local health care district.

A focal point in the definition of bank foundations' governance pertains to the local stakeholders who are called to appoint the members of the Board of Trustees. The foundation cannot take into account all the individual actors and entities in this group. For this reason, the law defines general characteristics that should guide choice, while the statutes can more specifically define the primary group of interest or the institution called to propose the candidates.

Within Italian bank foundations, good governance requires a multistakeholder approach in the composition of the Board of Trustees. This complex process takes into account the interests of the community. In this regard, mission stakeholders are not directly represented within the Board of Trustees, but their interests are guaranteed by a fair representation of the more general community interests. This governance system is transparent and prevents overlapping between the represented interests of the community and the grant-making activity on behalf of mission stakeholders.

Some studies of nonprofit boards have explained how the characteristics of the board and its members can be useful for good governance (Young 2011) and link to good performance (Brown 2005).

In Italian bank foundations, the general features of the board are fixed by law, and each statute can establish a group of stakeholders who can nominate members of the Board of Trustees. This group is composed of local stakeholders who live or have an indirect influence on the foundation's activities. This category of stakeholder should not be confused with mission stakeholders, who are the direct beneficiaries of the grant-making activity.

To understand the common entities engaged in the selection of members of the Board of Trustees, we analyzed the 88 statutes to identify these groups of interest. To simplify the analysis, we identified six groups of local stakeholders (Fig. 4.2): the assembly of original associates; the public sector; culture, education, and research groups; trade and professional associations; civil society; and other stakeholders.

In general, private and public organizations interested in the territory needs are taken in account. These entities appoint the Board of Trustees according to rotation criteria and choose people who preferably live in the territory where the foundation resides. Such appointment is not a representation of these entities' interests but rather an assembly of unique competences, knowledge, and experiences.

In most cases, there is a general reference to the organization called to choose the members; however, the organization specifies the person who has this task, for example, the president or the head of the entity.

The "assembly of original associates" occurs only in bank foundations with associative origins. In these foundations, approximately half the Board of Trustees is appointed by the assembly, without specific identification with local stakeholders.

In the "public sector" group, many different public organizations at different levels (municipal, provincial, regional, and governmental) can improve, influence, and inform the foundation's activity because they are involved in local social and environmental development.

Principal Entities in Public Sector Group

- Mayor of the city
- Municipalities
- Provincial committees
- Regional committees
- Ministry of economy or environment
- Union of Provinces

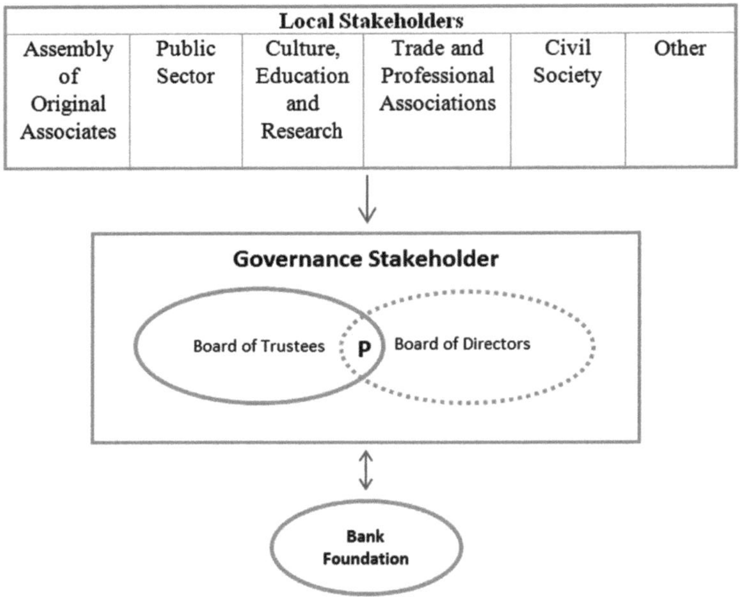

Fig. 4.2 Stakeholder and governance

The "culture, education, and research" group includes organizations that support society in the improvement of knowledge at different ages and levels. This group includes universities and other research institutions, as well as organizations that are called to diffuse culture in the local community.

Principal Entities in the Culture, Education, and Research Group

- Universities
- Schools of fine arts
- Higher education institutions
- Museums
- Libraries
- Conservatories
- Cultural foundations

The "trade and professional associations" stakeholder group comprises organizations that include professional, self-employed individuals in different industries such as commerce, advisory and building, and the labor unions.

Principal Entities in Trade and Professional Associations group

- Chambers of commerce
- Land reclamation authority
- Industrial unions
- Artisans confederations
- Farmers unions
- Association of architects, lawyers, or doctors
- Labor unions

"Civil society" is the broadest stakeholder group in terms of types of entities it comprises. Civil society includes entities (excluding public ones) that are involved in social development of territory, such as nonprofit organizations that are influenced by the actions of bank foundations but not in a direct way. For example, if the foundation decides to restore a painting in a church, the direct beneficiary is that specific church. However, the community at large, tourists, and the district church also indirectly benefit from this initiative.

Principal Entities in the Civil Society Group

- Volunteer organizations
- Health care sector
- Equal opportunities commission
- Blood donation association
- Other foundations
- Curia Romana or diocese
- Sports associations

The residual group of "other" includes the members chosen using the general aspect established by law but without a precise type of stakeholder group.

General Entities in the "Other" section

- People who have distinguished themselves in scientific or cultural fields of intervention.
- Public or private organizations of the local environment.
- People who can contribute to the foundation activity for the social and economic development of the territory.

4.2.2 Choosing Mechanisms of the Boards

As Young (2011, p. 576) notes, "voting mechanisms are devised for election of representatives from each group, just as shareholders in for-profit corporations are allowed to vote their shares."

In Italian bank foundations, the Board of Trustees is defined using four different approaches, or more often a hybrid of the following:

- Different categories of local stakeholders propose a list of candidates, and the expiring Board of Trustees chooses a member for each shortlist proposed.
- The Board of Trustees identifies the people to appoint in the local stakeholders' categories, whose interests are closely aligned with the bank foundation's mission.
- Local stakeholders directly designate the members of the Board of Trustees.
- The assembly of the original associates establishes the members of the Board of Trustees.

When the assembly of original associates exist, it constraints the development of an analytic stakeholder map. The assembly represents a general, local stakeholder, and the associates themselves are expressions of the local environment.

Ente Cassa di Risparmio di Firenze
Article 8—The Associates
The Associates of the Entity are ideally the successors of the founders of the Society of the Savings Bank.
Associates are members of the Organization having the established requirements. They cannot exceed the number of 160 members.
Associates must be citizens mainly residing in Florence and Tuscany; they can also be foreigners linked to the Tuscan society from long tradition.
They must have full civil capacity, be of undoubted moral integrity, and must occupy or have occupied enhancing functions in the cultural, economic, and social fields and therefore be sufficiently representative for personal gifts as part of business; administrative, and professional activities; study and research; artistic activities; and civil life.

When the foundation does not have an assembly form, the local stakeholder map can be drawn more completely. The statutes identify in a precise way the different entities called to make up the Board of Trustees. The statutes also identify the local stakeholders called to designate the members of the Board of Trustees and regulate the way they actually participate in the definition of this board. The law and the autonomy of the statutes make it possible to transparently outline the relationship between the bank foundation's governance and the territory. This is an essential element of good governance and provides a clear definition of the roles and responsibilities.

The composition of the Board of Trustees expresses a general interest that embraces the needs of the territory in which the foundation resides. The mixed-designation method shows different degrees of autonomy established by the statutes.

Members of the Board of Directors are designated by the Board of Trustees. The appointment of this board represents the mandate given to the Board of Trustees to identify the best professional skills and competences that will be useful to define strategies congruent with the interest of the territory. In this sense, the Board of Directors also represents the territory, though indirectly.

The president of the foundation symbolizes the operating unity of the organization. The president's functions are strictly linked to the normal conduct of the meetings, and this person is the legal representative of the foundation. The president is appointed by the Board of Trustees and can be confirmed only one time. The duration in this office, however, is variable and depends on the statutory provisions.

4.3 Mapping Stakeholders in Governance Foundations

In establishing the composition of the Board of Trustees, there are two basic principles regarding the characteristics of a member. He or she must be

- Representative of territory in an adequate and qualified manner, and
- Have professional skills, knowledge, and experience within the bank foundation's sectors of interest.

In addition to these criteria, which are strictly linked to the personal identity of the members, another general principle considers the equilibrium within the Board of Trustees. The representation of the local stakeholders must be balanced, and there cannot be one stakeholder category with a majority presence. The autonomy of the statutes must safeguard this sense of equilibrium, giving balanced power of designation to the different categories of local stakeholders.

To guarantee broader representation, a rotation or shift form of designation can be used within local stakeholder categories distinguished by a large number of constituents (e.g., local authorities).

The aim of this regulation is to prevent a situation in which a majority power of a group of local stakeholders can determine a permanent link between the bank foundation and defined interests of particular private or public organizations.

Considering the importance given by law to the local stakeholders in the composition of the Board of Trustees, it is important to examine the different weights given to the different stakeholder categories.

The law gives the statute the power to regulate these aspects in detail. Thus, to understand in depth the Italian bank foundations' governance, we analyzed the content of the statutes of the 88 Italian bank foundations. The overall picture that emerges shows aspects of foundations that statutes have regulated in a similar and sometimes very different way.

To collect the information needed for this research, we conducted a content analysis (Krippendorff 1980) of the statutes of all the bank foundations. Specifically, we coded qualitative information into categories, which provided quantitative data. With this analysis, we sought to identify the frequency with which the group of stakeholder would be called on to appoint new members to the Board of Trustees. A complete list of the content analysis units associated with the local stakeholders group appears in the Appendix (see Sects. A.3 and A.4). The selection of the cluster used is a result of discussion and consensus between the authors.

To ensure that we had the latest version of the statutes, we sought information (1) directly from the websites of foundations, (2) from the official website of ACRI, and (3) through requests sent to the secretaries of each foundation if information was not available online. Statutes collected are the most recent available at the time of writing for each foundation.

To accurately reflect the nature of the foundations, we account differently for bank foundations distinguished by an assembly form (42 foundations) and those not distinguished by an assembly form (46 foundations).

4.3.1 Local Stakeholders' Power of Designation in Bank Foundations Without an Assembly

In foundations that do not have an assembly, it is easier to identify more clearly the local stakeholders called to propose or choose members of the Board of Trustees. The categories used for the analysis are the same as those discussed in Sect. 4.2, with the addition of those designated directly by outgoing members of the Board of Trustees.

As Fig. 4.3 shows, the different stakeholder groups have different levels of power in designating members of the Board of Trustees. The most influential group is the public sector (38.73 %) (e.g., local authorities), followed by trade and professional associations (16.56 %); the Board of Trustees (15.07 %); culture, education, and research (11.83 %); civil society (10.71 %); and other stakeholders (7.10 %).

Table 4.5 presents a summary of the members chosen by the different categories of local stakeholders. The analysis accounts for both the size dimension and the geographical areas and underscores the importance of the public sector in each dimension. The table shows that trade and professional associations have significant power of designation in medium (21.50 %), medium-small (22.14 %), and small (18.42 %) bank foundations. Regarding geographical area, we note that the public sector is the most powerful in central Italy (48.91 %).

As Chap. 5 explains in greater detail, bank foundations' sectors of interest change every 3 years, while the members of the Board of Trustees hold office for longer periods. In this regard, the separation between the local stakeholders and the mission stakeholders that are the beneficiaries of the foundation activity is clear.

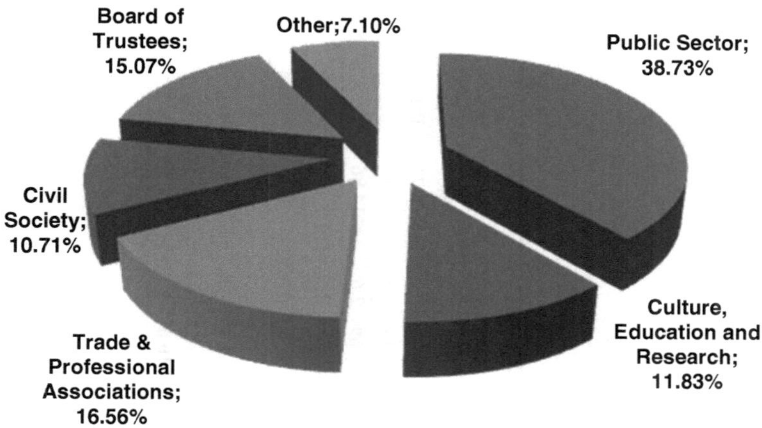

Fig. 4.3 Local stakeholders called to define members of the Board of Trustees

The general interests represented by the members of the Board of Trustees are an expression of the territory's needs, not those of a particular stakeholder.

4.3.2 Local Stakeholders' Power of Designation in Bank Foundation with an Assembly

For bank foundations with an assembly body, it is not as easy to gain a clear picture of the different weights given to the local stakeholders by the statutory autonomy. Figures 4.4 and 4.5 show cases with and without the assembly, respectively.

Usually, the power given to the assembly of original associates in choosing members of the Board of Trustees is slightly less than half the total members (48.82 %). Consistent with foundations that do not have an assembly, the public sector holds the most significant importance (21.33 %), followed by trade and professional associations (10.66 %); civil society (9.00 %); culture, education, and research (7.70 %); and finally the Board of Trustees and other (2.49 %).

As Fig. 4.5 shows, when the assembly is not considered, the different weights given to the different local stakeholders are clear. The ratios among the different local stakeholders are similar to the situation described in Sect. 4.3.1, the only exception being civil society, which, in the assembly form, has a higher percentage (17.59 %) than in the other foundations (10.71 %).

Table 4.6 shows that the stakeholders involved in the culture field hold greater power in the large foundations (12.28 %). Regarding the weight given to trade and professional associations, we note that in the northern region of Italy, the mean number of members is double that in the central region.

The impossibility of drawing a complete map of the local stakeholders in bank foundations with an assembly form gives an incomplete view of the actual

Table 4.5 Local stakeholders in foundations by size and geographical area for bank foundations without an assembly

	Public sector		Culture, education, and research		Trade and professional associations		Civil society		Board of Trustees		Other	
Size	Mean	%	Mean	%	Mean	%	Mean	%	Mean	%	Mean	%
Large	9.4	40.80	2.4	10.37	2.9	12.71	2.8	12.37	3.6	15.72	1.9	8.03
Medium-large	5.9	32.34	3.1	16.92	2.6	14.43	1.3	6.97	2.5	13.43	2.9	15.92
Medium	6.4	42.06	0.9	5.61	3.3	21.50	1.0	6.54	2.9	18.69	0.9	5.61
Medium-small	6.1	37.40	2.3	13.74	3.6	22.14	2.0	12.21	2.3	13.74	0.1	0.76
Small	4.3	39.47	0.9	7.89	2.0	18.42	1.9	17.11	1.3	11.84	0.6	5.26
Total	**6.8**	**38.21**	**2.1**	**11.67**	**2.9**	**16.34**	**1.9**	**10.69**	**2.6**	**14.86**	**1.5**	**8.03**
Geographical	Public sector		Culture, education, and research		Trade and professional associations		Civil society		Board of Trustees		Other	
area	Mean	%	Mean	%	Mean	%	Mean	%	Mean	%	Mean	%
North	7.1	37.92	2.2	11.58	3.1	16.44	2.1	11.24	3.1	16.61	0.8	6.21
Central	6.4	48.91	1.6	11.96	2.3	17.39	0.9	6.52	0.9	6.52	1.1	8.70
South and islands	5.7	31.75	2.1	11.90	2.7	15.08	2.0	11.11	2.3	12.70	3.1	17.46
Total	**6.8**	**38.21**	**2.1**	**11.67**	**2.9**	**16.34**	**1.9**	**10.69**	**2.6**	**14.86**	**1.2**	**8.23**

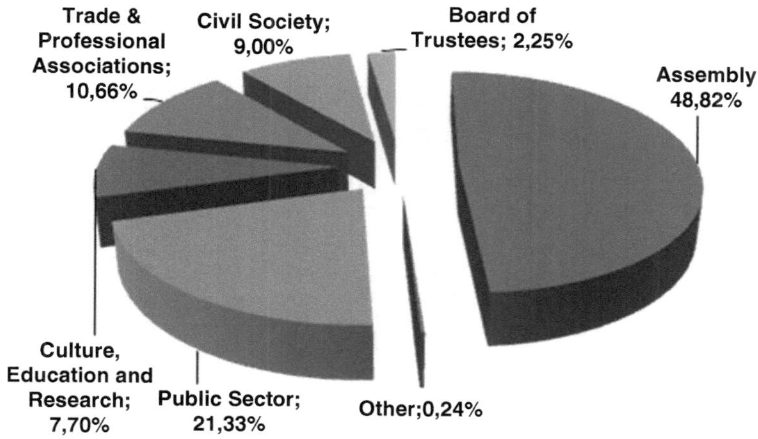

Fig. 4.4 Local stakeholders called to define members of the Board of Trustees, considering the assembly weight

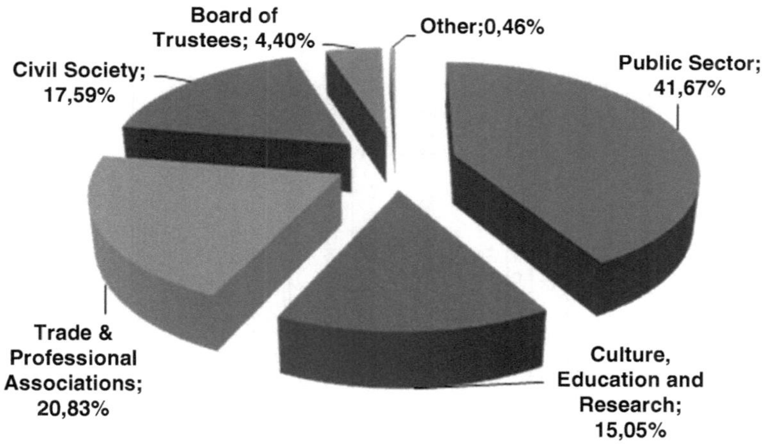

Fig. 4.5 Local stakeholders called to define members of the Board of Trustees, not considering the assembly weight

assignment of the designation power. The assembly might not transparently represent the interests of the territory. Indeed, with specific regard to the members chosen by the assembly, the statute does not establish which are the local stakeholders of interest for the bank foundation.

Table 4.6 Local stakeholders in foundations by size and geographical area in bank foundations with an assembly

Size	Assembly		Public sector		Culture, education, and research		Trade and professional associations		Civil society		Board of Trustees		Other	
	Mean	%	Mean	%	Mean	%	Mean	%	Mean	%	Mean	%	Mean N.	%
Large	11.2	49.12	4.4	19.30	2.8	12.28	1.4	6.14	1.8	7.89	1.2	5.26	1.2	0.00
Medium-large	12.2	50.00	5.3	21.92	1.7	6.85	2.8	11.64	2.3	9.59	0.0	0.00	0.0	0.00
Medium	10.8	48.77	4.2	18.85	1.3	5.74	3.5	15.57	1.8	8.20	0.6	2.87	0.6	0.00
Medium-small	8.8	49.69	4.4	25.16	1.3	7.55	1.3	7.55	1.4	8.18	0.3	1.89	0.3	0.00
Small	7.7	46.96	3.6	22.10	1.4	8.29	1.5	8.84	1.8	11.05	0.3	1.66	0.3	1.10
Total	**9.8**	**48.82**	**4.3**	**21.33**	**1.5**	**7.70**	**2.1**	**10.66**	**1.8**	**9.00**	**0.5**	**2.25**	**0.5**	**0.24**

Geographical area	Assembly		Public sector		Culture, education, and research		Trade and professional associations		Civil society		Board of Trustees		Other	
		%	Mean	%	Mean	%	Mean	%	Mean	%	Mean	%	Mean	%
North	10.4	47.87	4.2	19.34	1.4	6.56	3.2	14.75	1.9	8.85	0.6	2.62	0.0	0.00
Central	9.5	49.35	4.3	22.45	1.6	8.35	1.6	8.35	1.8	9.09	0.4	2.04	0.1	0.37
South and islands	N.A.													
Total	**9.8**	**48.8**	**4.3**	**21.33**	**1.5**	**7.70**	**2.1**	**10.66**	**1.8**	**9.00**	**0.5**	**2.25**	**0.0**	**0.2**

NA not applicable because there are no bank foundation with an assembly form in the south and islands region of Italy

4.4 Incompatibility and Conflicts of Interest

Incompatibility refers foremost to conflicting membership in the different bodies of the bank foundation (strategic, administrative, and control). A member of the Board of Trustees cannot be a member of the Board of Directors, and vice versa. At the same time, and for the same reason, a member of the assembly cannot be a member of either of the boards. The only exception is the president, who is in charge of both the strategic and administrative bodies and is the legal representative of the bank foundation.

This general principle does not impede members of the Board of Directors from attending the Board of Trustees meeting; however, they would have no voting rights in this meeting. In this regard, members of the administrative body can contribute to the discussion and provide support with regard to their specific knowledge of problems, particularly to help define the foundation's programs.

Beyond the notion of internal incompatibility, the statute can establish external incompatibility guidelines. The following list provides some examples of people who might represent an external conflict of interest:

- A parent or relative,
- An employee or advisor,
- A person involved in a local stakeholder group established by the statute,
- A member of another bank foundation board,
- A person without the personal characteristics specified by law,
- A member of the Board of Directors of the spin-off bank,
- A mission stakeholder, and
- A person who has damaged the foundation.

The general rule is that there cannot be an overlap between the foundation's interests and those of a member. A person holding a position on a board must be completely independent in carrying out tasks and ensuring transparent decisions.

At the time of initial assessment, the Board of Trustees must verify the members' qualifications and confirm that there are no conflicts of interest.

As Young (2011) observes, nonprofit boards are often affected by conflicts of interest (Jegers 2009) or "groupthink" (Leslie 2009), which can compromise the development of the nonprofit's functions or the correct use of funds. Within bank foundations, members of the boards work in the interest of the organization. It is considered a conflicting situation when a member's interests overlap with the bank foundation's interests—for example, when a member is called on to make a decision that directly or indirectly affects his or her job or personal concerns.

With regard to bank foundations' employees, they cannot carry out other activities that contradict the foundation's mission. Likewise, when an employee works for or is a volunteer in an organization that benefits from the foundation activity, they must disclose it.

Another important cause of conflict of interest regards asset management by qualified financial brokers (Legislative Decree no. 58/1998). The criteria for choosing this broker should be in the interest of the bank foundation and must discount any possible conflict of interest between the board members and the broker. In some cases, the foundation relies on an independent technical committee to choose the broker.

When there is a conflict of interest or an incompatibility, the member must disclose this to the body to which he or she belongs before a decision is made. If the conflict is of a temporary or unintended nature, the body (usually the Board of Trustees) decides on proper action or duration of suspension; if malicious, termination of board member status may result.

Conflict of Interest and the Code of Ethics
Fondazione CR Province Lombarde (Cariplo)
The Cariplo Foundation Code of Ethics applies to employees, coworkers, and members of the boards of the Foundation: its observance is an integral part of the contractual obligations. Anyone who provides a service for Cariplo Foundation is required to prove honest and transparent strategies, objectives, and operations; be effective and efficient in their work; be willing to work for discussion and learning; have no conflict of interest; be respectful of people and places in which he works; and be active in promoting the achievement of institutional mission and the advancement of social good. The conduct of each employee must safeguard the quality, efficiency, and not least the reputation of Cariplo Foundation, both in the workplace and outside of it. The Foundation focuses its activities on the people, enhancing their diversity and identifying the tools to develop their potential.

References

Barrett M (2001) A stakeholder approach to responsiveness and accountability in nonprofit organizations. Soc Policy J NZ 1(17):36–51

Bradshaw P, Murray V, Wolpin J (1996) Women on boards of nonprofits: what difference do they make? Nonprofit Manag Leadersh 6(3):241–254

Brown WA (2002) Racial diversity and performance of nonprofit boards of directors. J Appl Manag Entrep 7(4):43–57

Brown W (2005) Exploring the association between board and organizational performance in nonprofit organizations. Nonprofit Manag Leadersh 15:317–339

Donaldson T, Preston LE (1995) The stakeholder theory of the corporation: concepts, evidence, and implications. Acad Manag Rev 20(1):65–91

European Foundation Centre (2007) Principles of good practice. European Foundation Centre, Brussels

Glaser EL (2003) Introduction. In: Glaser EL (ed) The governance of non-for profit organizations. University Press, Chicago, pp 1–44

Jegers M (2009) Corporate governance in nonprofit organizations a nontechnical review of the economic literature. Nonprofit Manage Leadersh 20(2):143–164

Krippendorff K (1980) Content analysis. An introduction to its methodology. Sage, Beverly Hills
Leslie MB (2009) Conflicts of interest and nonprofit governance: the challenge of groupthink. Benjamin N Cardozo School of Law, Jacob Burns Institute for Advanced Legal Studies, Working paper no. 276, http://ssrn.com/abstract=1477553. Accessed 20 May 2013
Ostrower F, Stone MM (2006) Governance: research trends, gaps, and future prospects. In: Powell WW, Steinberg RS (eds) The nonprofit sector: a research handbook, 2nd edn. Yale University Press, New Haven/London, pp 612–628
Spear R, Cornforth C, Aiken M (2009) The governance challenges of social enterprises: evidence from a UK empirical study. Ann Public Coop Econ 80(2):247–273
Young DR (2011) The prospective role of economic stakeholders in the governance on nonprofit organizations. Voluntas 22(4):566–586

Chapter 5
Governance and Strategic Planning

5.1 The Key Role of Strategic Planning

In Italian bank foundations, the role of governance structure is crucial to ensure that asset management and grant-making decisions are congruent with the mission of the organization and the strategy it intends to adopt.

Governance puts attention on defining roles and responsibilities within the organization. It assigns to the board the responsibility of defining both the mission and the assets that promote its realization and assigns to management the duty to carry out the activities related to asset management and the pursuit of public purposes. Therefore, mission and goals are the strategic areas that involve the board, while action steps are developed by management (Dees et al. 2001).

Good governance depends on adequate governance tools. In this regard, the nonprofit literature highlights strategic planning as a key governance tool because it helps formalize strategy through action plans. In doing so, it helps the board think and act strategically and look to the future in a deliberate manner. More so than strategic planning per se, strategic thinking and acting are important (Bryson 1988).

Studies on the role of strategic planning in nonprofit organizations are not new. There is broad agreement that strategic planning is a critical component of good governance and management in nonprofits, and evidence shows that it has become a widespread and ubiquitous practice in recent decades (Bryson 2010).

In the past, the traditional practice has been to adjust programs in response to citizen demands for more services. This short-term perspective is no more satisfactory now. At the same time, the traditional attempt to respond to change after it occurs is inadequate. Providing services and financing them cannot be reliably executed by projecting past trends into the future.

Strategic planning—broadly understood as the set of approaches used to support decision making (Medley and Akan 2008)—helps nonprofit organizations respond to issues proactively and successfully optimize human and financial resources. In other words, it provides know-how that can be helpful to decision makers (Bryson et al. 2009). Its diffusion among nonprofit organizations, therefore, is not simply a

C. Leardini et al., *Board Governance in Bank Foundations*, Contributions to Management Science, DOI 10.1007/978-3-642-41306-3_5,

consequence of faddishness, coercion, or normative phenomena; instead, it often represents a way to promote strategic thinking, improve decision making, and increase organizational performance. In this sense, Bryson (2010) shows that strategic planning typically works well and produces positive results.

In addition, the absence of profit (Anthony and Young 1999; Moore 2000) increases the importance of strategic planning as a governance tool for nonprofit organizations because planned actions should produce more satisfactory results (Porter 1980).

In general terms, strategic planning is a process concerned with strategy, which involves defining long-term goals and identifying the polices needed to achieve them (McHatton et al. 2011). As Bryson (2004, pp. 27–28) states, strategic planning

> is meant to help public and nonprofit organizations (and communities) create public value through meeting their mandates and fulfilling their missions. In order to do so it must produce fundamental decisions and actions that shape and guide what the organization is, what it does, and why it does it. Producing those decisions requires an interconnected set of activities that organize participation, create ideas for strategic action, build a winning coalition, and implement strategies.

Strategic planning implies an evaluation of values, goals, and priorities for courses of action that ensure the organization's ability to add public value.

Therefore, strategic planning is a process governed by the board that facilitates an understanding of the forces that drive issues, explores the feasibility of different options and their likely consequences, and stimulates the evaluation of costs and risks associated with various alternatives (Poister 2010). Such a process can be represented as a sequence of intertwined decisions that flow from strategy formulation to strategy realization, for both asset management and grant-making activity (Fig. 5.1).

The first step of the process is clarification of the foundation's mission and values that provide the social justification for its existence (Freeland 2002). Drawing from its mission and values, strategic planning contributes to the identification of appropriate goals that are legitimate and sustainable. The second step of the process requires a careful analysis of the internal and external environment (SWOT analysis [strengths, weaknesses, opportunities, and threats]); this provides the board with a sense of how things stand and contextualizes the objectives pursued. A proper strategy can then be formulated as a pattern of decisions that determines and reveals the foundation's purposes, produces policies and plans to achieve them, and identifies the nature of the contribution it intends to make in the interest of the territory (Andrews 1980). After the strategy has been formulated, it should be made explicit through action plans for the medium-long period. Those plans allow the board to clarify strategy and to translate the broad vision of the foundation into more operational terms. The next step of the process is the allocation of financial resources, which should be consistent with strategic priorities and long-term objectives (Mara 2000). After the allocation of resources, budgets can be formulated and formalized. They must identify short-term goals to be pursued, funds to be used, and activities to be performed.

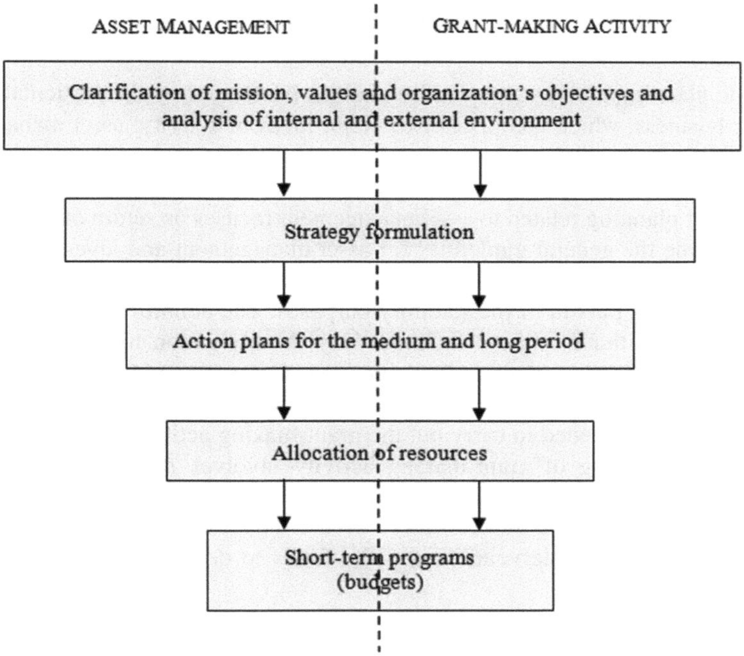

Fig. 5.1 Strategic planning process in bank foundations

Strategic planning plays a key role in the management of bank foundations to ensure that the funds are employed coherently with the mission. It provides a basis for developing programs, monitoring progress in actions, and assessing whether the results achieved both in asset management and in grant-making activity contributed to the social and economic development of the territory.

Strategic planning turns the philanthropic activity carried out by bank foundations into a sort of strategic philanthropy, which replaces the stereotypical models of the "good father" or "enlightened banker" (Boesso et al. 2011).

With regard to strategic planning, the analysis of the Italian bank foundation experience shows that this process is expressly stipulated by law, involves the Board of Trustees and the Board of Directors, and is conditioned by the management of assets donated for public purposes.

5.2 What Is Strategic Planning?

Strategic planning activity in bank foundations is affected by the particular nature of their business, which comprises two major areas of activity: asset management and grant-making activities. In terms of content, then, it is possible to distinguish two matters that must be planned.

Strategic planning related to asset management focuses on return on investment. It must define the general guidelines for asset management and investment policy with respect to the constraint placed by the law according to which assets are fully committed to the pursuit of the statutory purposes. The definition of strategies and action plans for the future are influenced by the obligation to comply with the prudential management of risk (diversification of investments) aimed to preserve the value of assets and to ensure that capital investments are appropriate and provide the funds needed to carry out the grant-making activity.

Strategic planning of grant-making activity involves maximizing the social value for the territory. It must identify the sectors in which the foundation preferentially will operate, the stakeholders' needs, their priority of satisfaction, the general guidelines of intervention, and the funds to devote to different areas of grant-making activity.

Therefore, strategic planning is twofold, but it would be a mistake to consider the two planning activities separately.

As discussed in Chap. 2, asset management and grant-making activities are complementary and interdependent and require strategic coordination by a single body with a unitary view.

Grant-making activities, which are the core business of foundations, depend financially on asset management. The effective management of assets ensures the availability of funds to finance social activities. In this sense, choices about the management of assets must be consistent with the needs (timing and amounts) of the grant-making activity. At the same time, grant-making goals must be connected with the financial resources that asset management can make available. It follows that strategic planning must consider jointly both asset and grant-making management (Leardini 2005).

Strategic planning requires a broad vision of the mission as a whole, a thorough control of internal and external factors that could affect both asset management and grant making, a comprehensive strategy, and long-range planning for the two areas of activity. Unified, concurrent, and strategically coordinated decisions are fundamental conditions for ensuring the durability of the foundation, particularly "when grant-making policy may limit the asset management and conversely when a bad-management of the assets may jeopardize the institutional goal of bank foundations" (Alberti 2002, p. 6).

In this sense, planning in bank foundations should take the form of integrated strategic planning—that is, the formulation of strategic asset allocation objectives in accordance with grant-making activity needs. In line with this condition, returns on investments should be appropriate to support the grant-making activity, which requires careful analyses of needs and proper identification of the priorities of recipients to identify consistent actions.

Strategic planning managed in a unified way becomes a tool for translating the mission into action (Bryson 1988; Freeland 2002), allocating limited available funds (Mara 2000), and building consensus among various stakeholders (Bradach and others 2008).

Changes in the external environment increase the significance of strategic planning. In a changing environment, bank foundations need to be clear about the risks associated with asset management, the needs of the territory, their varying priorities, and the interventions enacted to realize their goals. This reinforces the importance of strategic planning being carried out by a board with a broad vision of the foundation and its social function.

5.3 Who Is in Charge of Strategic Planning?

In general terms, strategic planning can involve a large group of people. In some cases, the decision-making process can be conducted exclusively by the board of the organization, while in other cases, the process can be implemented by a committee, which increases consensus about the objectives pursued and the activity conducted (Arif and Smiley 2004; Bradach et al. 2008; Crittenden and Crittenden 1997; Crittenden et al. 2004; Moxley 2004).

European Foundation Centre Principle no. 2 (2007) indicates that the presence of an identifiable decision-making body represents good governance practice within foundations.

In Italian bank foundations, strategic planning involves both the Board of Trustees and the Board of Directors. Their roles and responsibilities take into account the notion that asset management and grant-making activity are strongly complementary and interdependent, thus requiring strategic coordination.

The Board of Trustees is responsible, by law and statutory definition, for the direction function. It must ensure a functional link between the logic of maximizing returns on assets and the social mission of the bank foundation. Therefore, it must define programs, priorities, and goals and identify the guidelines for asset management (Article 4 of Legislative Decree no. 153/1999). In general, it is in charge of "a deliberative, disciplined effort to produce fundamental decisions and actions that shape and guide what an organization (or other entity) is (its identity), what it does (its strategies and actions), and why it does it (mandates, mission, goals, and the creation of public value)" (Bryson 2010, pp. 256–257).

The Board of Trustees is representative of the local community in which the foundation operates and is responsible for achieving social purposes and economic development of the territory. As described in Chap. 4, the process of composing the Board of Trustees aims to better understand and represent the most relevant and prioritized needs of the community so that the foundation uses its funds properly. The duty of planning long-term strategies makes it clear why the law and the statutes require that board members have a high degree of professionalism, experience, and expertise appropriate to the areas of intervention and the other activities of the foundation.

All these elements considered together—decision-making body, responsibility to the territory, composition, and professional requirements—reflect the logic of the provision that puts the Board of Trustees in charge of strategic planning, with the duties of affirming the mission, developing the key objectives of the foundation, and ensuring that strategies and plans lead to the attainment of the goals for both asset management and the grant-making activity.

A Look to the Statutes—Board of Trustees' Tasks

The analysis of the statutory provisions of the 88 Italian bank foundations confirms the importance that the definition of the strategic guidelines for the long-term period is made by the Board of Trustees.

With particular regard to asset management strategic planning 86 cases recognize that the Board of Trustees is responsible for defining the main asset management and investment policy guidelines. Forty four statutes underscore the strategic significance of such decisions, provided that asset management strategic planning is reserved exclusively for the Board of Trustees, while the Board of Directors lacks even proposal rights. However, 7 Italian bank foundations grant the Board of Trustees only the more restricted task of deliberating on or approving guidelines for asset management rather than defining them. This finding calls for some consideration of the terminology used, which could reveal how the law has been incorporated and translated into statutes. The law states that it is the duty of the Board of Trustees *to define* the main lines of asset management; the use of this active verb clearly delineates the role assigned to this board.

With regard to grant-making strategic planning, 75 statutes recognize that the Board of Trustees has the duty of defining multiannual plans to ensure effective interventions and the efficient allocation of resources within the relevant sectors.

Strategic planning also involves the Board of Directors. Although this board does not have the function of planning strategy, it has the duty (*Atto di Indirizzo* no. 186/1999) of translating the strategic guidelines stated by the Board of Trustees into operational short-term programs to be transmitted to management for implementation. While the Board of Trustees puts emphasis on setting the general framework and guidelines for subsequent decision making, the Board of Directors focuses on the sustainable actions within the constraints of mandates, missions, goals, and strategies. In this sense, the Board of Directors identifies short-term programs that detail interventions, amounts, and beneficiaries.

In addition, the law assigns to the Board of Directors proposal functions under the programs, priorities, and objectives set by the Board of Trustees. Members of the Board of Directors, therefore, can take part in the Board of Trustees' meetings, though without a voting right, and support the decision-making process through their own professionalism and expertise. In this way, the committee style of strategic planning (Mintzberg 1994) is realized, which favors a shared model of creating and enacting the strategic function.

The parameters of the proposal function must be correctly identified. To propose does not mean to define, and it is clear that the law wanted to delimit the Board of Directors' power over the foundation's strategy. As a consequence, the Board of Directors cannot define strategic guidelines and multiannual plans; that remains the task of the Board of Trustees. Indeed, being responsible for defining purposes, mandates, goals, issues, and strategies cannot mean merely approving a multiannual planning document drawn up by the Board of Directors. If so, there would be a transfer of functions and responsibilities, which entails the risk of reducing the focus on long-term planning, such that strategic planning becomes a short-term management tool rather than a multiannual strategic view.

A Look to the Statutes—Overlapping Functions

Although the law provides for different roles and responsibilities of the boards, it is often difficult to separate clearly the duties pertaining to the Board of Trustees from those allocated to the Board of Directors. It depends on the way the statutes specify the functions of the two bodies and the competences and skills that their members possess.

The statutes of the 88 Italian bank foundations show that, in some cases, there is an allocation to the Board of Directors of tasks that should be the sole responsibility of the Board of Trustees. More specifically, Boards of Directors are sometimes assigned direction-related functions that go far beyond the power of suggestion and purpose recognized by law for this board.

Analysis of statutes shows this anomaly especially with regard to the activity of multiannual strategic planning. Of the 88 bank foundations, 64 statutes recognize that the Board of Trustees has the duty to plan grant-making activity in the long term, bearing in mind the available resources deriving from asset management and the needs of the community. When multiannual planning language is stipulated in the Board of Trustees' functions, 61 statutes establish that the board is in charge of *defining* programmatic guidelines and multiannual planning. In only 3 cases, the board *approves* the multiannual planning proposed by the Board of Directors. In general, then, the policy-making body is responsible for the multiannual strategic planning function, whereas the administrative body serves in a more short-term, proposal-related capacity.

Although the statutes give general attention to the multiannual planning function, the statutory analysis indicates somewhat limited attention to the multiannual planning document. Only 32 statutes make specific reference to

(continued)

(continued)

it. The presence of a multiannual planning document is particularly low in small bank foundations, which is likely a result of their greater focus on short-term strategies. When the multiannual planning document is mentioned, the Board of Trustees is explicitly called on to approve it in 19 cases. Eight statutes specify that the document should be drawn up by the Board of Directors and approved by the Board of Trustees, which seems to reduce the decision-making weight of the latter. This situation demands particular attention because it creates the risk that the document will include only a short-term (annual) perspective that characterizes the Board of Directors' work. Moreover, these statutory provisions might end up transferring functions and responsibilities between internal bodies of the foundation, which would represent a misapplication of the functional separation established by law.

Article 20 of the Statute of the *Ente CR di Firenze* exemplifies such risk, stating that the Board of Directors defines the strategies and objectives to be pursued and the lines and priorities regarding the management and use of assets.

5.4 How Is Strategic Planning Formalized?

Strategic planning is formalized through three different documents that consider jointly both asset management and grant-making activity (Fig. 5.2):

- The multiannual planning document.
- The annual planning document.
- The analytical plan for deliberations.

Every 3 years, the Board of Trustees identifies within the multiannual planning document the areas of intervention (relevant sectors), describes the strategic objectives to pursue within them, and estimates the expected funds necessary to realize such objectives.

Every year, the Board of Directors prepares an annual planning document that must be approved by the Board of Trustees. The document describes for each sector of intervention the objectives to pursue during the next year and the funds that predictably will be allocated to them.

Finally, the Board of Directors identifies the analytical plan for deliberations with regard to the annual articulation of the activities planned for the next year.

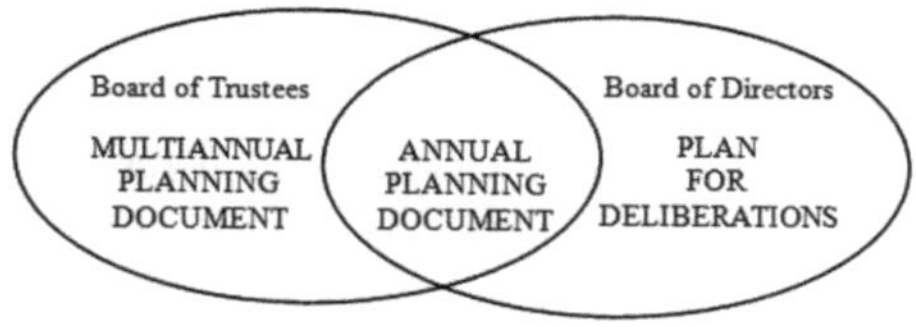

Fig. 5.2 Strategic planning documents

5.4.1 *The Multiannual Planning Document*

Strategic planning activity implies an emphasis on long-term goals and strategies. It mainly consists of a multiannual planning document that outlines guidelines for strategies, objectives, priority areas of intervention, asset management, and investment policies to accomplish in the future.

The Board of Trustees draws up the multiannual planning document every 3 years. Changes in environment require the multiannual planning document to be continuously monitored, reviewed, and updated to be consistent with the changing needs of the territory, almost one a year.

The main purposes of the document are to ensure the best use of funds and the effectiveness of interventions, the observance of a principle of economy, and compliance with predetermined prudential risk criteria to preserve the value of the assets and to obtain an adequate return.

Because the document is, by definition, a multiannual forecast, it should not include the specifics of a short-term plan, in which objectives, interventions, and timelines are detailed in a more definitive way. Instead, it should be more general, though not generic.

Its content should reflect the different steps in which the process of strategic planning is developed, starting with the description of the mission and ending with the allocation of financial resources, always remembering to jointly consider both asset management and the grant-making activity. The multiannual planning document can be structured in five sections, as detailed in the next box.

Section One: Mission, Values, and Bank Foundation's Goals

- Mission: Promoting the social and economic development of the territory, beyond a profit-making intent
- Values: Promoting socially oriented values in the pursuit of public interests
- Goals: Ensuring an adequate return on investments and maximizing the outcome for the territory in the relevant sectors of intervention

(continued)

(continued)

Section Two: External and Internal Environment

External Environment
- Opportunities and threats facing the organization in planning asset management
- Characteristics of the financial market and a combination of risk and return on investments
- Changing needs and priorities of the territory
- Strategies and activities of institutional partners and other foundations

Internal Environment
- Strengths and weaknesses affecting the organization
- Professionalisms and experiences of the bank foundation's members

Section Three: Strategy
- Relevant sectors of intervention
- Prevalence of grant-making or operating activity
- Collaboration with other organizations
- Beneficiaries of the grants provided
- Use of instrumental enterprises
- Degree of risk and expected return on investments
- Shareholding in spin-off banks

Section Four: Plans of Action
- Guidelines of investment and divestments policy
- Type of investment, characteristics in terms of duration, amount, expected return, and risk
- General criteria for divestments
- Scale of priorities in interventions (parameter coefficients)
- Criteria for selecting projects

Section Five: Allocation of Resources
- Total amount of available resources
- Allocation of resources by sector of intervention
- Amounts devoted to annual, multiannual, and continuative interventions

5.4.1.1 Section One: Mission, Values, and Bank Foundation's Goals

The first section introduces the foundation's mission, values, and goals. For this purpose, the information contained within the statutes could be used because the aims of the organization are already delineated here.

Their common origin by law renders all bank foundations' missions similar to one another. They all hold the exclusive purpose of promoting social and economic development of the territory, beyond the profit-making intent, and emphasize socially oriented values that determine their action in the pursuit of public interests. The section should also indicate the objectives to pursue during the next 3 years.

Regarding asset management, the objectives can be summarized in the following general terms: to ensure an adequate return on investments and to maintain (and increase when possible) the assets' value. To operationalize this general purpose, multiannual planning documents should contain a more detailed description of the objectives pursued.

The Case of the Fondazione CR Pisa

The Foundation intends to pursue the following objectives concerning the asset management activity during the period 2013–2015:

- Make available each year 10.5 million euros for projects within the statutory areas of intervention.
- Make provisions equal to 35 % of the operating surplus to maintain the assets' value.
- Make provisions in support of the volunteers, in accordance with the law.
- Contain asset management and administrative costs within the maximum of 1.1 million euros.

The objectives of the grant-making activity can be summarized in the following general terms: to maximize the value for the territory in the relevant sectors of intervention. Defined in this way, however, the objective is too broad and general to be useful in the planning process.

To facilitate the identification of more specific purposes to pursue within the different areas of intervention and to operationalize them, the general mission of the foundation can be articulated in specific submissions for each sector in which the organization chooses to operate. In this way, there is a clear connection among the mission as a whole, the specific submission for the sector, and the objectives the foundation intends to pursue within it.

The Case of the Fondazione CR Padova e Rovigo

Mission

To support projects that contribute to improving the quality of life and promote economic development of the territory of Padua and Rovigo, through dialogue and collaboration with local institutions, nonprofit organizations, and other entities.

(continued)

(continued)

Submission for the Research Sector
Help the local research sector compete with the best international scientific realities, assuming that an improvement of the research quality favors the social and economic development of the territory.
Objectives for the Research Sector
The mission highlights three fundamental aspects:

1. Raising the quality of research.
2. Disseminating results for the social and economic development of the territory.
3. Being internationally competitive.

From these aspects, the strategic objectives the Foundation wants to pursue within the Research sector are derived:

1. Promote the quality of research and scientific production.
2. Favor the implementation of the research results.
3. Promote the internationalization of the research institutions operating within the territory.

5.4.1.2 Section Two: External and Internal Environment

Bank foundations tend to retain their historical traditions. As a consequence, they usually pay attention to the needs to which they have always responded. However, this approach limits their ability to understand developments and changing needs over time.

Therefore, it is important to monitor the external environment to better understand the evolving contexts in which bank foundations operate. Attention paid to the changing needs of territory allows bank foundations to improve the effectiveness and efficiency of their operations and to avoid the risk of being self-referential in developing the grant-making activity. To this end, it is important to develop a fruitful discussion with the key stakeholders to ensure a sharing of the objectives pursued and a deeper knowledge of the social reality in which the foundation operates.

The analysis of the external environment is also fundamental to understanding the opportunities and threats that face the organization when planning asset management. To decide whether to adopt a conservative or an aggressive asset management policy, a careful investigation of financial markets and future scenarios is required to identify the most appropriate combination of risk and return that is consistent with the grant-making needs.

The analysis of future scenarios allows the foundation to simulate the expected income and gains arising from the financial portfolio during the next 3 years, which represents the main source of funds to finance grants and disbursements.

The Case of *Fondazione CR La Spezia*
Expected income of the Foundation's financial portfolio for the years 2011–2013

Income statement (thousands of euros)	2011 forecast	2012 forecast	2013 forecast	2011–2013 average
Dividends and similar income	4,997	7,139	7,378	6,505
Intesa San Paolo	*3,482*	*4,255*	*4,642*	*4,126*
CR La Spezia	*0*	*1,329*	*1,329*	*886*
CDP	*100*	*100*	*100*	*100*
Other	*1,415*	*1,455*	*1,307*	*1,392*
Interests and similar income	169	97	85	117
Financial current assets	*148*	*69*	*52*	*89*
Trade and cash	*21*	*28*	*33*	*27*
Revaluation of available-for-sale investments	1,897	1,951	2,020	1,956
Revenue	**7,063**	**9,187**	**9,484**	**8,578**

The analysis of internal environment characteristics highlights the strengths and weaknesses of the foundation. A central element of this analysis is the identification of professional skills and experience attributes that members of the foundation possess or should possess. The achievement of institutional goals requires a thorough knowledge of the needs of the territory and a deep understanding of market mechanisms.

5.4.1.3 Section Three: Strategy

According to the mission, values, objectives, and environment, bank foundations should identify their strategy for the next 3 years, always taking into account the deep linkages between asset management and grant-making activity.

Defining strategy requires the identification of a set of basic elements that are fundamental for achieving social and economic development of the territory—the general and ultimate purpose of bank foundations. Some examples of such basic choices include:

- Relevant sectors of intervention, among those admitted by law. The choice requires a thorough knowledge of the characteristics of the territory and its main needs and is influenced by size and geographical location of foundation.
- Prevalence of grant-making or operating activity. The Board of Trustees should clarify whether the foundation chooses to be a charity organization that disburses

contributions to those who require them or, on the contrary, assumes the responsibility for its own projects.

- Collaboration with other organizations. Bank foundations must decide whether to carry out their policies within a single agency or combine their interests and resources with other organizations (private or public institutions) and operate in partnership with them.
- Beneficiaries of the grants provided. Among the nonprofit entities operating within the territory, the Board of Trustees must identify those that can better foster the cultural, social, and economic growth of the local community.
- Use of instrumental enterprises for the implementation of the statutory purposes.
- Degree of risk and expected return on investments deriving from asset management that are considered congruent with the characteristics of grant-making activity.
- Shareholding in spin-off banks.

The Case of Fondazione CR Pisa

General Strategies and Intervention Policies

The Foundation's activity will pursue the following aims:

- Confirm its function as a modern and flexible tool for the economic and social development of the territory; propose itself as a cultural and operating model; and promote dialogue and collaboration with other organizations, associations, and institutions.
- Maintain a constant and close contact with the authorities and institutions of the territory; seek, where possible and appropriate, their collaboration in implementation of programs to obtain the participation and empowerment of the entire community.
- Create a structured planning of own projects and interventions, if necessary with the collaboration of other institutions, with the specific aim to avoid duplication of initiatives and the consequent waste of resources.
- Realize mainly large-scale projects, focusing on a limited number of initiatives to ensure the maximum effectiveness of the institutional activity.
- Play an active role in the management, promotion, and enhancement of the interventions, also through the establishment of specific instrumental entities.

5.4.1.4 Section Four: Plan of Action

After the strategy has been clarified, broad-scope plans of action need to be identified for the next 3 years.

With reference to asset management activity, the multiannual planning document should outline the guidelines of investment and divestment policy. More specifically, it should focus on the type of investment and its characteristics in terms of duration, amount, expected return, and risk. In the same way, the plan should specify general criteria for divestments, to satisfy the grant-making needs without compromising asset value maintenance.

With reference to grant-making activity, an essential element for the multiannual planning document is the scale of priorities the foundation must follow when it intervenes in favour of the territory within the chosen sectors. Currently, the identification of priorities consists merely of the choice of relevant areas of intervention among those indicated by law. Indeed, no multiannual planning document contains an indication of the hierarchy of priorities of intervention.

Identification of the priorities leads to the formalization of the criteria the foundation uses to select projects submitted by the territory.

Clear plans of action, drawn up from the stated objectives, make the strategy the Board of Trustees intends to pursue within the different areas of intervention more transparent and lead to better identification of the short-term objectives by the Board of Directors (Fig. 5.3).

5.4.1.5 Section Five: Allocation of Resources

The reasons for allocating financial resources are twofold: the satisfaction of the needs of the territory and, the preservation of asset value. It is, therefore, necessary to coordinate the allocation of funds for the next 3 years so that both investments and disbursements are consistent.

Because the funds that will be available for the next 3 years (the period referred to in the multiannual planning document) are not known, the Board of Trustees must be careful in its decision making. It must appeal to the professional qualifications and experiences of its members and to the support of study commissions and committees of scientific and technical evaluation.

With reference to grant-making activity in particular, the multiannual planning document should indicate not only the total amounts to be disbursed over the next 3 years but also their allocation by sector of intervention, distinguishing, when possible, among annual, multiannual, and continuative interventions.

The Case of *Fondazione Padova e Rovigo*

The allocation of the expected financial resources for the period 2010–2012 is as follows:

Sector of intervention	Expected amounts for the triennium	%
Scientific research	28,000,000	19
Education	31,000,000	21

(continued)

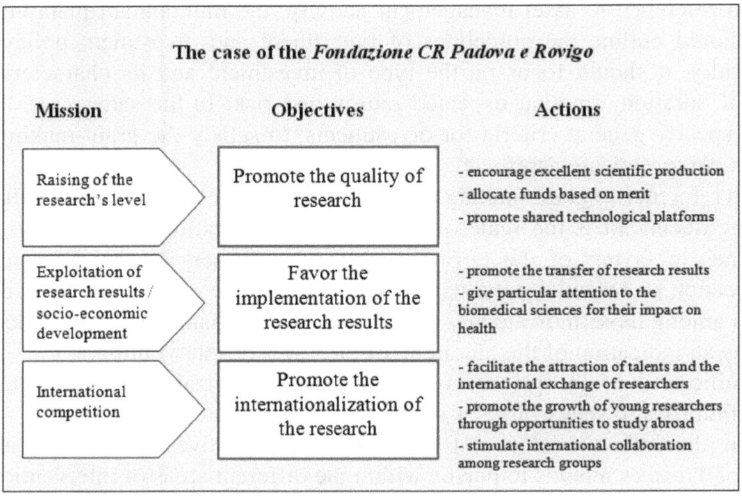

Fig. 5.3 The plan of action of the Fondazione CR Padova e Rovigo

(continued)

Sector of intervention	Expected amounts for the triennium	%
Art and culture	24,000,000	16
Health and environment	29,000,000	19
Social assistance	33,000,000	22
Total amount for relevant sectors	**145,000,000**	**97**
Other sectors	5,000,000	3
Total amount of funds for grant-making activity	**150,000,000**	**100**

If properly structured, the multiannual planning document offers a benchmark with which to compare the results the foundation achieves. Consequently, it allows for an evaluation of the congruence between the purposes stated and the actions. Indeed, if the basic assumption of strategic planning is that planned actions should produce satisfactory results, this does not mean, however, that planning alone is sufficient to ensure a priori the effectiveness and efficiency of interventions.

To facilitate the verification of results achieved and to make explicit the indicators based on which the work of the Board of Directors (and management) will be assessed, the multiannual planning document may provide some indicators. These can be helpful in guiding the grant-making activity in a more effective and efficient way.

The Case of *Fondazione CR Padova e Rovigo*
Indicators for Research Sector

	Results	Indicators
Outcome	New businesses/services	Number of start-ups/spin-offs
	Increase in the productivity of research	Number of scientific publications (with impact factor and citation index)
	Increase in innovations	Number of patents (national and international)
	Economic impact	Revenue deriving from patents
		Direct impact on production, sales, and markets
	Incentive of research	Number of new research projects
	Improvement of social welfare	Impact of the research within the territory (improvement of quality of life, social enjoyment of goods and services)
	Employment increase	Impact on local employment
Activity	Employment increase	Personnel full-time employed in the project
	Increase of research activity	Number of researchers employed in the year
	Increase of researchers' number	Number of added researchers
		Number of researcher added in the year
	Increase of highly specialized education	Number of PhD grants
	Greater internationalization	Percentage of foreign researchers
	Increase in scientific disclosure	Number of seminars, workshops, and conferences
	Increase of tools and resources	Number and value of new equipment
	Increase/begin new collaborations	Number of research institutions involved in the project
	Incentive to technology transfer	Number of enterprises involved in the project
Efficiency	Project activity	Co-funding by third-parties
	Researchers activity	Overall financing/researchers number
	Resources increase	(Total revenue—foundation's grants)/total revenues
	Cost reduction	Incidence of operating expenses on the project
	Efficient use of resources	Number of researchers daily using equipment
		Utilization rate of equipment
	Management efficiency	Ratio between researchers and total personnel

Furthermore, to be an instrument capable of providing the Board of Directors with guidelines that are easy to implement, the multiannual planning document should be sufficiently general, though not generic. Otherwise, strategic planning activity loses its benefits. At the same time, the Board of Directors gains some autonomy in defining purposes and policies of intervention that goes against the principle of functional separation required by law.

5.4.2 The Annual Planning Document

The annual planning document specifies objectives, tools, and operational guidelines for implementing the multiannual planning document over the next year.

Unlike the multiannual planning document, the law requires the annual planning document. Each bank foundation must adopt it for the next year by the month of October and then forward it to the supervising authority. The document is usually prepared by the Board of Directors and must be approved by the Board of Trustees, which then verifies its coherence with the multiannual planning document.

The presence of this gray area in which the duties of the Board of Directors seem to overlap with those of the Board of Trustees can create critical issues in the relationship between the two bodies. For this reason, to avoid confusion and conflict, it is important that the foundation clearly identifies through the statutes the roles and responsibilities of the boards.

While the multiannual planning document outlines the allocation of the expected funds on a triennial basis, the annual planning document specifies in detail the actions to carry out within the different sectors.

The annual planning document specifies for the short-term period (the next year) the strategic guidelines fixed within the multiannual planning document. Based on the latter, the former recalls the areas of intervention, subdivides the amounts allocated over the next 3 years, and provides a more detailed plan of action for the immediate future. The aim of the document, therefore, is to identify which projects and interventions the bank foundation will reasonably engage in during the next year and the funds that will likely be allocated to it.

The general structure of the document does not differ significantly from that already described for the multiannual planning document. However, because its aim is to operationalize the long-term plans stated by the Board of Trustees, the annual planning document is usually articulated by sectors of intervention and focused on them.

After a brief and general reference to the context in which the foundation operates, its mission, the objectives pursued, and the manner of intervention to highlight the deep connection with the multiannual planning document, the annual planning document should provide a forecast of the funds available for grant-making activity.

To this end, a thorough knowledge of asset management is required. The board is called to revise the forecasts of assets and operating surplus for the next year made in the multiannual planning document and to update them in accordance with the changing environment. The expertise and professional requirements mandated by the statutes for the members of the boards should ensure that such forecasts are reasonably reliable.

After the forecasts have been verified, and eventually revised, the expected funds available for grant-making activity should be subdivided among the sectors of intervention following the guidelines established by the Board of Trustees within the multiannual planning document.

The Case of *Fondazione CR Forlì*

The Foundation provides a table that highlights the main elements that will form the operating surplus and the financial resources available for disbursements in the coming year.

	Budget 2013
Income from asset management activities	6,740,665
Dividends	6,348,725
Interests and similar income	411,718
Revaluation of available for sale investments	–
Costs:	2,147,886
Payments and refunds for the boards	*490,000*
Personnel costs	*870,313*
Consultant services	*63,000*
Asset management costs	*19,000*
Depreciation	*33,173*
Other costs	*672,400*
Income tax expense	55,800
Operating surplus	**11,297,422**
Allocation to mandatory reserve	2,259,484
Available surplus	**9,037,938**
Allocation to voluntary fund	461,865
Allocation to asset's value maintenance fund	1,176,073
Available funds	**7,400,000**

Next, the plan is presented for the allocation of funds among relevant sectors and other sectors in which the foundation has decided to operate in the course of next year.

	Budget 2013
Relevant sectors	
Art, cultural and artistic activities	2,500,000
Research	1,000,000
Public health	800,000
Local development	900,000
Voluntary activities, philanthropy and charity	1,000,000
Total amount relevant sectors	6,200,000
Admitted sectors	
Social assistance	400,000
Sport and recreation	350,000
Education, learning and training	300,000
Environmental protection and quality	150,000

(continued)

(continued)

	Budget 2013
Total amount admitted sectors	1,200,000
Total amount	**7,400,000**

When the financial resources have been identified, the annual planning document focuses on each area of intervention to set up specific plans of action for the next year.

The different sections of the document (one for each area of intervention) should specify the particular submission for the sector, the objectives the foundation intends to pursue within it, the program guidelines for such area, and the manner of intervention (e.g., grants or own projects, collaboration with other entities) established by the Board of Trustees within the multiannual planning document.

The Case of Fondazione CR Padova e Rovigo

The Foundation allocated €28 million in the triennium to the scientific research sector. The annual plan presents a detailed allocation of this amount for the period, with €9 million being the amount to be allocated to the sector in 2012. The plan specifies the guidelines to be followed in the use of such funds.

Submission for the Research Sector

Help the local research sector compete with the best international scientific realities, considering that an improvement of the research quality favors the social and economic development of the territory.

Objectives for the Research Sector

- Promote the quality of research and scientific production.
- Favor the implementation of the research results.
- Promote the internationalization of the research institutions operating within the territory.

Guidelines

- Encourage excellent scientific production.
- Allocate funds based on merit, using the method of peer review.
- Promote shared technological platforms within the territory.
- Promote the transfer of the research results.
- Give particular attention to the biomedical sciences for their impact on health.

(continued)

(continued)

- Facilitate the attraction of talent and the international exchange of researchers.
- Promote the growth of young researchers through opportunities to study abroad.
- Stimulate international collaboration among research groups.

Manner of Intervention
Own projects:

- Announcement aimed at supporting the best research projects in the following research areas: biomedical, sciences and technology, humanities, and social sciences.
- Support of grants for PhD courses.
- Support to youth entrepreneurship and transfer of technology and expertise to the enterprises.
- Promotion of international exchanges and training periods abroad for young researchers.

Third-party projects:

- Acceptance of proposals coming from the territory that are congruent with the aforementioned guidelines

This sort of information allows for a better understanding of the strategic context in which the action plans for the next year are placed.

A brief but exhaustive description of the project areas the foundation aims to support within the different sectors should then be presented. This presentation should include the salient features of the projects the foundation intends to support and finance, which may be accompanied by an indication of the amounts allocated to them.

The Case of Fondazione CR Verona
Education, Learning, and Training Sector
New projects for 2013 (total available funds: €3.1 million)

- At a time of severe crisis in the labor market, the Foundation considers as a priority the creation of employment opportunities for young people. The Foundation aims to support employment centers accredited by the Region. In particular, programs will be evaluated that aim to provide and/or extend the technology park and laboratory equipment. Accredited nonprofit

(continued)

(continued)

training organizations will also be supported in the realization of training courses aimed at providing employment.

- The Foundation will evaluate experimental initiatives aimed at promoting direct contacts among graduates, PhD students, postdoctoral students, and enterprises to increase the competitiveness and to enhance innovation. It will also support formative experiences of mentoring between people who prematurely stopped working and young graduates to increase their specialization and organizational skills. The foundation ensures to both subjects, because of their potential disadvantage, a minimum accompanied income.
- Tools and equipment. The Foundation will support partially the primary and secondary schools in the purchase of computer equipment that is functional to teaching. The Foundation will also support the purchase of furniture and equipment for schools. Maximum amount that can be requested: 30,000 Euros per project.

5.4.3 The Analytical Plan for Deliberations

The analytical plan for deliberations concludes the strategic planning process, highlighting the detailed programs that management must implement during the next year. The document is the sole responsibility of the Board of Directors, which has the duty to operationalize the guidelines expressed within the annual planning document through specific programs of intervention.

When the Board of Directors specifies the programs for the grant-making activity, it should consider some relevant issues:

- The identification of programs, for both asset management and grant-making activity, should not contrast with the guidelines established in the multiannual and annual planning document.
- The asset management programs must evaluate the ability of financial investments to generate cash as well as the timing and certainty of its generation to ensure the financial coverage of the projects that the board resolves to achieve.
- The allocation of expected funds among the different project areas within a sector should be consistent with the priorities stated by the Board of Trustees, which has a thorough knowledge of the needs of the territory.
- The evaluation of different alternatives of intervention having the same priority within the sector should consider the risk associated with their realization.
- The programs must take into account the eventuality that some projects may involve the foundation for more than the next year.

Therefore, the analytical plan for deliberations identifies the specific projects the foundation will carry out during the next year, specifying spending limits for each.

The document consists of several sheets, one for each project in which the foundation intends to engage. The content of the sheets can be summarized as follows:

- A brief description of the project that highlights its aims and content;
- The total amount of funds allocated to the project and its deadline;
- If the project is developed through announcements, the subjects admitted to the presentation of applications for the grants and those that are excluded, specifying their characteristics (e.g., nature of the institution, activity carried out, seat, geographical area of operations);
- The arrangements for payment of contributions (e.g., one disbursement, more disbursements in the course of time);
- The formal requirements that the application must meet (e.g., documentation to be attached, expiration date);
- The general criteria that will be used in the evaluation of applications submitted by the territory (e.g., consistency with the foundation's statutes and regulations, adherence to local needs and impact on the local community in terms of number of beneficiaries, involvement of other institutions operating within the territory, expected ability to complete the project);
- The procedure that will be used in the evaluation and selection of the applications received (e.g., formal admissibility of the application, verification of its consistency with the aims of the project, assessment of the merits of the application).

All information contained in the plan must then be submitted to the management so that it can implement the decisions of the boards and focus on operational aspects in running the organization. Management, in particular, must issue the announcements, select the applications received on the bases of criteria identified by the Board of Directors, and disburse the funds to the beneficiaries.

To facilitate control over its activity, the analytical plan for deliberations should also contain some formal elements that must be quoted within the intervention sheets compiled by management, such as the number that identifies the practice, the reference year, the sector and subarea of intervention, the amount, and date of the resolution. This plan makes it possible to relate the activities of the management to the programs established by the board and to more easily verify the results achieved.

5.5 Strategic Planning and Boards' Responsibilities

Strategic planning is essential for developing programs, monitoring progress in actions, and assessing results to ensure that the funds are achieving the greatest impact for the social and economic development of the territory.

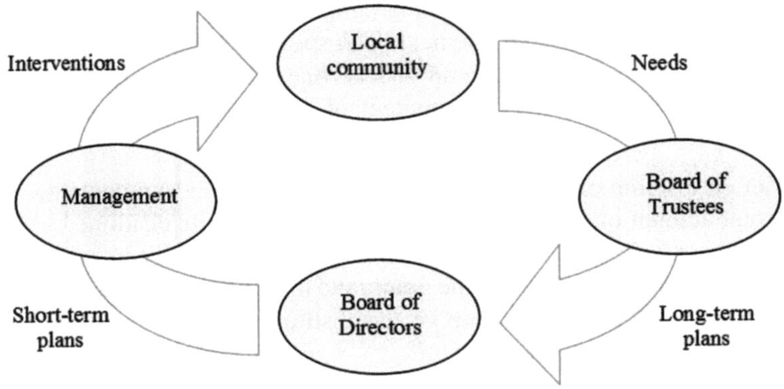

Fig. 5.4 Boards' responsibilities

Deep strategic planning steps and documentation help outline the responsibilities assigned to the different governance participants and their ability to translate missions into objectives and strategies.

In the absence of a profit aim, good strategic planning and good governance represent two crucial elements to ensure that the needs of the territory are adequately recognized and translated into strategies and actions of the foundation. As Young (2011, p. 571) contends, the mission of the organization gives the boards a "fiduciary responsibility wherein board members understand their role to be trustees of the greater good addressed by the organization's mission."

Strategic planning and the clear identification of the boards' and management's roles favor a proper allocation of responsibility to the different organs that contribute to the pursuit of the mission (Fig. 5.4).

Because bank foundations operate in the exclusive interest of the territory, their main responsibility is to deliver interventions to the local community. In the local community, we found that local stakeholders are called to represent the territory's needs and that mission stakeholders are the beneficiaries of the grant-making activity. As we noted in Chap. 4, these two groups are, respectively, indirectly and directly involved in the bank foundation's activity.

The definition of responsibilities starts with the Board of Trustees, which is responsible for identifying the needs of the local community, assigning them a hierarchy that is consistent with their priority, setting general guidelines for interventions, and allocating funds through multiannual planning documents. The main challenge is to ensure the coherence between the needs of the territory and the policies of the bank foundation. It is important, therefore, that the board is an expression of the local stakeholders. The board is also responsible for reviewing the results achieved and for revisiting the mission every 3 years (Dees et al. 2001).

After strategies have been identified, the Board of Directors, together with the Board of Trustees, has the duty of identifying various short-term (the next year) measures to achieve the goals, obtain an adequate return on investments, and allocate the expected funds within the different sectors following the guidelines established by the multiannual planning document. To this end, the two boards should be supported in their work by the competences, expertise, and proficiencies of their members.

The Board of Directors identifies more analytical programs to operationalize the guidelines stated in the annual plan. In this sense, its responsibility is to define timing and methods of intervention, formalizing them into the plan for deliberations.

Finally, management is responsible for the operational aspects and financial matters in running the organization (Anheier 2005). Consequently, it implements programs and delivers grants or own projects to the territory in accordance with the short-term programs established by the Board of Directors. Good governance implies that the boundary between the boards' responsibilities and management's responsibilities is clearly defined. As Hudson (1999) highlights, the boards have the duty to ensure that the organization is well managed, but not to manage it. Sometimes, however, board and management roles overlap, and the identification of responsibilities becomes difficult. Good governance in bank foundations means that management runs the organization within the guidelines established by the boards and implements them through actions.

As Fig. 5.4 shows, the local community is the final point of reference in assessing whether interventions delivered by the bank foundation effectively satisfy the needs of the territory.

When there is no consistency between interventions and needs, it is important to check which step of the circular process has failed and to make the necessary adjustments and properly assign accountability for the failure (Leardini 2005).

In this way, the philanthropic activity of bank foundations can become a strategic philanthropy, which makes Italian bank foundations one of the most important examples of "Philanthropication thru Privatization" (Salamon 2010).

References

Alberti GB (2002) La determinazione dei risultati della gestione delle fon-dazioni bancarie. RIREA, Rome

Andrews KR (1980) The concept of corporate strategy. RD Irwin, Homewood

Anheier HK (2005) Nonprofit organisations: theory, management, policy. Routledge, London

Anthony R, Young DW (1999) Management control in nonprofit organization. McGraw Hill, New York

Arif M, Smiley FM (2004) Baldrige theory into practice: a working model. Int J Edu Manage 18 (5):324–328

Boesso G, Cerbioni F, Menini A, Parbonetti A (2011) Governo e prestazioni nelle fondazioni di origine bancaria. Il Risparmio 1(1):5–34

Bradach JL, Tierney TJ, Stone N (2008) Delivering on the promise of nonprofits. Harv Bus Rev 86 (12):88–97

Bryson JM (1988) A strategic planning for public and non-profit organizations. Long Range Plann 21(1):73–81

Bryson JM (2004) Strategic planning for public and nonprofit organizations, 3rd edn. Jossey-Bass, San Francisco
Bryson JM (2010) The future of public and nonprofit strategic planning in the United States. Public Adm Rev 70:255–267
Bryson JM, Crosby BC, Bryson JK (2009) Understanding strategic planning and the formulation and implementation of strategic plans as a way of knowing: the contributions of actor-network theory. Int Public Manage J 12(2):172–207
Crittenden WF, Crittenden VL (1997) Strategic planning in third sector organizations. J Manage Issues 9(1):86–103
Crittenden WF, Crittenden VL, Stone MM, Robertson CJ (2004) An uneasy alliance: planning and performance in nonprofit organizations. Int J Organ Theory Behav 7(1):81–106
Dees JG, Emerson J, Economy P (2001) Enterprising nonprofits. A toolkit for social entrepreneurs. Wiley, New York
European Foundation Centre (2007) Principles of good practice. European Foundation Centre, Brussels
Freeland C (2002) Strategic planning: SRA's approach. J Res Adm 33(2):59–65
Hudson M (1999) Managing without profit: the art of managing third-sector organizations. Penguin, London
Leardini C (2005) L'amministrazione della fondazione bancaria. Cedam, Padua
Mara C (2000) A strategic planning process for a small nonprofit organization: a hospice example. Nonprofit Manage Leadersh 11(2):211–223
McHatton PA, Bradshaw P, Gallagher PA, Reeves R (2011) Results from strategic planning process. Benefits for a nonprofit organization. Nonprofit Manage Leadersh 22(2):233–249
Medley B, Akan OH (2008) Creating positive change in community organizations: a case for rediscovering Lewin. Nonprofit Manage Leadersh 18(4):485–496
Mintzberg H (1994) The rise and fall of strategic planning: reconceiving roles for planning, plans, planners. Free Press, New York
Moore MH (2000) Managing for value: organizational strategy in for-profit, nonprofit, and governmental organizations. Nonprofit Volunt Sec Q 29:183–204
Moxley DP (2004) Factors influencing the successful use of vision-based strategy planning by nonprofit human service organizations. Int J Organ Theory Behav 7(1):107–132
Poister TH (2010) The future of strategic planning in the public sector: linking strategic management and performance. Public Adm Rev 70:246–254
Porter ME (1980) Competitive strategy. Free Press, New York
Salamon LM (2010) Philanthropy: Italy's Charitable Alchemy. In: Proceedings of the 10th Foundation's day, Fondazioni: eredi di comunità, figlie del Parlamento, Rome, 10 June 2010
Young DR (2011) The prospective role of economic stakeholders in the governance of nonprofit organizations. Voluntas 22:566–586

Erratum to: Board Governance in Bank Foundations

Chiara Leardini, Gina Rossi, and Sara Moggi

Erratum to:
C. Leardini et al., *Board Governance in Bank Foundations,* Contributions to Management Science, DOI 10.1007/978-3-642-41306-3

Owing to an unfortunate error, this book was initially published with the wrong copyright year 2013. This has been corrected in the new printing, in the online edition and in the metadata. The correct copyright year is 2014.

Chiara Leardini (✉) • Sara Moggi
University of Verona, Via Montanari 9, 37129 Verona, Italy
e-mail: chiara.leardini@univr.it; sara.moggi@univr.it

Gina Rossi
University of Udine, Via Tomadini 30/A, 33100 Udine, Italy
e-mail: gina.rossi@uniud.it

C. Leardini et al., *Board Governance in Bank Foundations,* Contributions to Management Science, DOI 10.1007/978-3-642-41306-3_6,

Appendix

A.1 Relevant Financial Statement Items (2012)

This section provides the relevant financial statement items of Italian bank foundations, focusing on 2012. The data are aggregated by size of bank foundations.

C. Leardini et al., *Board Governance in Bank Foundations*, Contributions to Management Science, DOI 10.1007/978-3-642-41306-3,

Table A.1 Relevant financial statement items – large bank foundations (2012)

Foundation name	Net assets (€)	Dividends and similar income (€)	Financial investments (€)	Current financial assets (€)	Interests and similar income (€)	Net revaluation of financial assets (€)	Operating surplus (€)	Boards' payments (€)
C.R. Province Lombarde	6,550,955,301	48,369,823	1,833,300,058	5,483,243,185	2,433,635	−9,891,160	278,326,227	−1,838,021
San Paolo di Torino	5,621,663,693	115,754,275	3,565,850,085	2,857,870,818	714,738	−1,090,559	195,982,915	−1,290,864
C.R. Verona, VI, BL, AN	2,658,394,150	14,298,710	2,846,119,667	71,915,662	24,503,027	3,958,968	51,338,832	−2,045,468
C.R. Torino	1,916,583,003	40,986,737	2,543,622,146	37,675,760	15,710,697	−43,285,528	12,153,707	−1,766,528
C.R. Padova e Rovigo	1,745,077,193	49,826,417	1,475,679,110	748,170,803	847,777	11,831,662	58,331,896	−1,462,087
Roma	1,444,712,622	46,340,960	1,537,266,325	1,004,476	2,019,611	3,986	35,063,055	−2,162,034
C.R. Cuneo	1,330,164,010	26,008,197	1,213,671,546	150,962,491	12,105,211	−17,266,037	32,055,835	−1,191,041
C.R. Firenze	1,304,571,348	49,732,207	1,157,506,729	125,742,886	2,823,534	−49,119	49,788,071	−1,151,783
C.R. Lucca	1,182,732,873	16,658,637	1,128,506,927	94,620,641	24,927,328	−3,001,255	41,805,237	−514,123
C.R. Genova e Imperia	1,012,613,126	75,073,525	1,412,150,020	9,692,968	1,142,938	0	67,203,323	−1,301,028
Banco di Sardegna	874,777,758	16,694,892	879,269,892	23,388,923	10,096,895	2,595,230	28,433,162	−1,031,582
Cassamarca	868,407,202	357,973	812,170,548	14,885,580	2,402,295	−9,893,417	2,209,035	−951,985
C.R. Parma e Busseto	833,500,241	22,041,480	936,603,970	28,047,694	2,839,999	−1,310,347	20,502,429	−441,382
C.R. Modena	825,004,991	23,401,674	697,684,705	190,644,425	6,989,312	2,739,569	39,884,949	−714,558
B.M. Lombardia	801,059,861	11,280,962	702,622,791	112,909,959	3,933,748	−761,392	11,269,232	−1,665,827
C.R. Bologna	756,716,175	17,517,078	1,218,623,496	3,968,216	141,526	−606,970	3,750,762	−1,493,570
C.R. Bolzano	731,497,545	8,123,042	562,795,500	105,623,512	6,639,687	948,776	15,016,178	−644,915
Monte dei Paschi di Siena	672,998,021	116,511	1,120,409,224	51,148,276	3,810,008	−157,515,861	−193,713,850	−1,676,407
Total	**31,131,429,113**	**582,583,100**	**25,643,852,739**	**10,111,516,275**	**124,081,966**	**−222,593,454**	**749,400,995**	**−23,343,203**

Table A.2 Relevant financial statement items – medium-large bank foundations (2012)

Foundation name	Net assets (€)	Dividends and similar income (€)	Financial investments (€)	Current financial assets (€)	Interests and similar income (€)	Net revaluation of financial assets (€)	Operating surplus (€)	Boards' payments (€)
C.R. Perugia	581,024,824	3,816,000	66,810,773	233,532,450	6,189,160	1,401,538	13,841,277	−570,394
C.R. Pisa	530,694,977	2,693,517	601,203,986	3,183,443	17,268,538	190,693	17,613,779	−628,299
C.R. Di Trieste	447,765,897	3,050,788	431,351,511	11,925,717	1,251,944	−1,897,370	1,114,174	−908,684
C.R. Forlì	433,278,852	6,560,927	234,641,530	213,097,549	710,083	−148,261	17,571,702	−452,110
C.R. Trento e Rovereto	377,510,666	8,438,071	280,477,820	79,962,664	2,208,212	−18,028,995	−2,846,308	−469,145
Piacenza e Vigevano	372,164,429	2,556,192	347,753,029	2,546,810	9,925,114	2,149,192	8,126,090	−409,868
C.R. Pistoia e Pescia	347,487,632	5,657,055	183,800,654	163,422,474	7,341,964	−151	11,959,565	−402,038
Venezia	328,546,685	8,712,604	220,819,273	90,326,559	473,950	−12,495,096	6,430,829	−894,534
C.R. Alessandria	323,148,235	4,119,399	218,464,952	29,513,432	4,430,375	−11,004,074	14,241,114	−1,039,411
C.R. Carpi	319,246,229	2,323,295	263,961,544	9,979,504	5,257,954	−1,151,760	7,049,562	−430,493
C.R. Pesaro	276,247,007	9,586,108	248,577,066	39,167,679	1,743,449	0	12,017,818	−295,806
C.R. Macerata	236,004,188	9,815,485	185,322,811	60,192,737	1,828,083	481,371	9,805,196	−413,159
M. Bologna e Ravenna	224,282,088	10,643,643	202,120,464	22,456,904	2,659,079	861,609	11,654,320	−625,175
C.R. Udine e Pordenone	220,250,043	6,198,184	174,950,853	71,554,725	3,021,427	452,230	11,788,773	−732,370
C.R. Biella	217,837,525	5,276,773	121,471,230	80,098,027	2,488,871	−5,017,954	5,850,681	−306,468
C.R. Pescara e LA	209,825,086	224,475	6,261,959	171,491,397	11,413,695	−4,512,838	4,117,450	−308,407
C.R. Tortona	209,196,050	219,010	89,157,290	104,363,365	2,851,271	2,617,746	9,459,960	−200,123
Total	**5,654,510,413**	**89,891,526**	**3,877,146,745**	**1,386,815,436**	**81,063,169**	**−46,102,120**	**159,795,982**	**−9,086,484**

Table A.3 Relevant financial statement items – medium bank foundations (2012)

Foundation name	Net assets (€)	Dividends and similar income (€)	Financial investments (€)	Current financial assets (€)	Interests and similar income (€)	Net revaluation of financial assets (€)	Operating surplus (€)	Boards' payments (€)
C.R. Livorno	208,366,802	2,335,395	141,741,184	5,077,833	4,006,434	220,422	6,542,808	−250,513
C.R. Asti	204,491,034	8,690,655	194,451,256	3,000,000	1,223,822	−842,931	6,643,034	−620,619
C.R. La Spezia	200,564,133	4,400,204	120,940,737	83,919,400	499,727	−154,693	3,218,465	−611,125
C.R. Ascoli Piceno	191,700,071	213,919	84,244,392	95,073,455	22,610	2,582	6,113,821	−348,599
C.R. Terni e Narni	186,647,484	2,252,710	125,357,772	22,032,005	4,123,988	1,480,125	7,024,377	−208,556
C.R. Ferrara	182,367,210	106,000	199,988,302	0	84,836	0	849,215	−115,192
C.R. Savona	178,785,064	4,171,634	77,952,472	0	2,916,359	0	10,708,664	−329,539
C.R. Gorizia	171,582,874	3,407,434	122,321,566	45,897,762	577,151	−1,500,000	6,010,296	−294,438
C.R. San Miniato	163,769,382	0	142,787,385	0	1,050,213	−11,369,282	0	−372,795
C.R. Teramo	162,659,517	780,972	139,097,862	28,998,170	1,618,765	735,252	4,371,932	−582,373
C.R. Imola	162,642,052	2,790,469	151,459,286	79,100,421	3,955,611	−1,716,689	5,850,229	−466,495
C.R. Fano	161,598,256	1,904,854	137,249,897	6,173,183	3,329,846	352,172	4,960,612	−252,227
C.R. Ravenna	156,199,200	11,052,022	126,692,448	23,149,654	794,931	388,983	12,926,630	−589,98
C.R. Reggio Emilia	154,637,960	1,073,535	154,835,004	9,919,891	142,691	−3,997,991	−3,866,634	−330,732
C.R. Volterra	151,363,000	66,948	101,877,033	30,561,810	1,265,824	−244,734	1,941,971	−299,034
C.R. L'Aquila	137,902,159	919,091	86,024,102	45,096,758	2,351,743	998,166	4,307,498	−335,929
C.R. Rimini	137,364,808	106,000	141,689,648	7,405,896	631,189	−79,783	417,019	−284,981
C.R. Carrara	131,805,343	2,003,607	94,853,789	30,271,854	1,071,572	−22,414,129	4,057,716	−372,956
Total	**3,044,446,349**	**46,275,449**	**2,343,564,135**	**515,678,092**	**29,667,312**	**−26,773,248**	**82,077,653**	**−6,076,103**

Table A.4 Relevant financial statement items – medium-small bank foundations (2012)

Foundation name	Net assets (€)	Dividends and similar income (€)	Financial investments (€)	Current financial assets (€)	Interests and similar income (€)	Net revaluation of financial assets (€)	Operating surplus (€)	Boards' payments (€)
M. Parma	126,860,247	0	43,779,270	44,631,661	6,219,769	0	5,304,296	–263,607
Banco di Sicilia	123,037,916	449,943	121,827,028	1,643,565	1,659,585	0	–2,649,006	–906,641
C.R. Mirandola	122,615,896	362,360	27,247,247	97,059,815	2,481,050	24,680	5,140,976	–111,287
C.R. Cesena	120,835,056	3,156,135	121,597,138	1,995,486	36,654	0	3,161,975	–188,200
C.R. Puglia	120,161,697	0	120,150,539	10,950	5,706,470	0	4,605,042	–344,810
Banco di Napoli	118,568,933	900,375	108,960,460	0	2,966,748	–1,084,000	2,799,206	–498,301
C.R. Vercelli	112,544,159	1,076,852	84,787,272	30,268,469	1,990,739	–617,817	3,651,002	–241,783
C.R. Jesi	104,325,991	4,486,135	106,513,836	1,154,231	1,111,513	0	4,374,739	–493,958
C.R. Rieti	101,021,905	1,646,417	66,960,369	13,630,958	1,529,529	0	2,949,653	–449,933
C.R. Prato	92,405,319	355,265	68,900,143	24,942,404	1,259,522	0	3,934,452	–210,854
C.R. Fermo	91,508,942	128,343	80,381,660	10,930,199	395,996	0	578,888	–259,279
C.R. Chieti	89,343,330	2,000,000	77,168,471	1,500,000	59,461	0	933,838	–356,401
C.R. Foligno	88,955,561	101,214	548,370	69,228,199	1,914,096	94,963	5,592,554	–288,805
C.R. Fabriano e C.	81,801,208	392,962	46,632,320	31,967,737	1,813,017	277,176	1,837,492	–181,069
C.R. Vignola	79,619,573	43,546	9,478,520	69,640,804	1,345,357	0	2,223,499	–222,773
C.R. Calabria e Lucania	76,852,266	159,000	6,889,382	70,917,545	3,456,096	0	3,288,514	–312,352
B.M. Lucca	75,481,348	1,632,320	47,494,226	27,387,044	758,975	0	2,575,627	–278,080
Total	**1,725,939,348**	**16,890,867**	**1,070,416,108**	**496,909,067**	**34,74,577**	**–1,304,998**	**50,302,747**	**–5,608,133**

Table A.5 Relevant financial statement items – small bank foundations (2012)

Foundation name	Net assets (€)	Dividends and similar income (€)	Financial investments (€)	Current financial assets (€)	Interests and similar income (€)	Net revaluation of financial assets (€)	Operating surplus (€)	Boards' payments (€)
C.R. Spoleto	73,075,344	1,082,043	25,702,475	13,038,922	1,141,220	548,768	2,265,296	−206,349
C.R. Orvieto	67,503,833	949,933	23,259,099	46,103,264	501,740	0	2,197,980	−165,425
C.R. Cento	55,639,861	1,276,005	44,419,538	9,173,214	355,113	77,189	1,158,000	−187,432
B.N. delle Comunicazioni	55,492,926	1,848,324	13,560,051	76,603,607	1,126,934	698,059	1,666,188	−249,721
C.R. Fossano	51,502,581	2,885,045	47,479,588	6,854,985	201,493	−670,620	2,209,416	−280,981
C.R. Civitavecchia	47,456,845	1,384,013	39,149,480	0	462,297	0	4,077,268	−434,702
C.R. Saluzzo	42,187,787	963,350	35,680,606	5,050,523	311,205	−135,936	873,775	−174,182
C.R. Salernitana	39,614,297	53,729	5,854,918	29,042,066	461,543	21,413	457,231	−96,909
C.R. e B.M. Lugo	36,232,977	1,077,310	25,372,314	0	154,219	0	1,712,325	−229,979
C.R. Viterbo	35,984,581	602,589	13,028,988	26,291,217	9,875	20,406	2,562,496	−208,862
C.R. Savigliano	35,033,886	795,939	30,331,535	6,101,562	181,108	434,506	1,035,223	−62,878
B.M. Foggia	32,633,599	242,316	31,376,073	0	1,059,675	0	1,258,179	−105,595
C.R. Loreto	29,941,318	1,139,378	9,776,368	19,129,237	15,022,084	−177,241	1,002,087	−117,204
C.R. Città di Castello	27,837,781	52,478	20,880	6,110,791	463,510	44,505	371,997	−34,345
C.R. Bra	25,909,789	308,404	23,457,972	1,277,572	89,696	2,169	66,284	−135,015
B.M. e C.R. Faenza	17,432,487	463,278	16,855,316	0	91,685	0	444,929	−49,972
B.M. Rovigo	6,910,549	25,110	6,708,879	220,000	227,809	0	101,122	−58,419
Monte di Pietà di Vicenza	1,731,364	111,316	1,353,641	0	6,812	0	88,277	−15,530
Total	**682,121,805**	**15,260,560**	**393,387,721**	**244,996,960**	**21,868,018**	**314,998**	**23,548,073**	**−2,813,500**

A.2 Relevant Financial Statement Items (2011)

This section provides the relevant financial statement items of Italian bank foundations, focusing on 2011. The data are aggregated by size of bank foundations.

Table A.6 Relevant financial statement items – large bank foundations (2011)

Foundation name	Net assets (€)	Dividends and similar income (€)	Financial investments (€)	Current financial assets (€)	Interests and similar income (€)	Net revaluation of financial assets (€)	Operating surplus (€)	Boards' payments (€)
C.R. Province Lombarde	6,449,077,428	63,768,916	1,861,005,990	5,374,353,089	2,146,397	−7,789,376	−6,866,451	−2,589,028
San Paolo di Torino	5,559,321,938	134,768,647	3,624,318,037	2,809,089,345	818,755	−12,010,630	171,211,272	−1,627,042
C.R. Verona, VI, BL, AN	2,647,721,664	55,718,670	3,048,499,731	153,609,997	26,143,462	−255,847,714	70,927,401	−2,308,150
C.R. Torino	1,914,152,262	82,309,504	2,721,394,944	135,146,880	42,015,596	−59,207,791	6,985,302	−1,783,599
C.R. Padova e Rovigo	1,733,413,920	62,106,072	1,499,046,393	792,548,286	2,465,773	−25,816,894	37,165,577	−1,410,863
Roma	1,432,440,553	44,189,005	1,552,613,631	27,700,096	718,436	−3,986	40,152,601	−1,847,909
Monte dei Paschi di Siena	1,331,066,074	125,548,097	1,624,116,137	851,325,737	15,992,572	−163,978,595	−331,742,555	−2,037,654
C.R. Cuneo	1,318,944,468	28,834,546	1,121,912,457	204,857,848	11,942,632	−17,068,289	30,089,787	−1,259,013
C.R. Firenze	1,294,613,734	44,368,343	1,157,105,999	144,267,580	1,794,874	−916,207	39,607,024	−1,130,884
C.R. Lucca	1,174,371,826	20,842,681	1,043,649,034	155,422,288	24,517,859	−2,726,661	35,357,364	−518,602
C.R. Genova e Imperia	1,059,479,438	72,083,869	1,412,154,746	0	3,539,090	0	66,646,944	−1,437,618
C.R. Parma e Busseto	936,650,345	32,748,993	1,045,207,207	19,492,587	2,513,147	−4,949,560	28,012,125	−471,361
Cassamarca	867,229,034	4,691,726	744,889,451	5,444,176	2,676,449	−13,407,580	−5,399,899	−1,014,059
Banco di Sardegna	863,776,240	12,249,860	857,122,691	25,746,151	10,582,903	111,028	24,615,628	−974,373
C.R. Modena	814,754,106	36,412,806	623,824,268	250,731,962	11,489,628	−11,787,809	44,303,012	−729,024
B.M. Lombardia	796,981,160	11,484,611	675,159,656	122,720,408	1,922,655	−836,801	8,988,164	−1,655,759
C.R. Bologna	755,794,142	30,774,222	1,281,336,808	22,307,860	1,155,294	29,972	−32,920,452	−1,624,046
C.R. Bolzano	721,141,882	8,469,110	602,735,254	169,770,059	6,158,892	493,487	12,951,570	−621,991
Total	**31,670,930,214**	**871,369,678**	**26,496,092,434**	**11,264,534,349**	**168,594,414**	**−575,713,406**	**240,084,414**	**−25,040,975**

Table A.7 Relevant financial statement items – medium-large bank foundations (2011)

Foundation name	Net assets (€)	Dividends and similar income (€)	Financial investments (€)	Current financial assets (€)	Interests and similar income (€)	Net revaluation of financial assets (€)	Operating surplus (€)	Boards' payments (€)
C.R. Perugia	661,501,167	9,284,012	426,136,141	265,112,668	1,602,365	−13,637	4,820,172	−697,026
C.R. Pisa	524,530,157	4,521,054	627,661,032	3,009,093	19,123,685	246,178	24,701,309	−374,928
C.R. Di Trieste	445,489,804	6,465,295	398,345,187	28,078,016	1,297,256	633,086	7,854,790	−901,986
C.R. Forlì	429,764,511	9,464,665	226,610,480	217,856,813	1,058,504	−484,713	9,212,864	−477,581
C.R. Udine e Pordenone	400,212,822	8,026,042	348,812,286	85,631,477	1,592,232	−454,627	12,176,754	−798,918
C.R. Trento e Rovereto	380,356,974	12,169,032	282,803,612	86,329,181	8,417,736	−3,069,315	14,150,223	−494,949
Piacenza e Vigevano	369,989,584	4,781,360	345,425,640	21,355,278	10,477,649	−25,748,850	9,575,416	−417,134
Venezia	366,077,039	12,461,435	318,750,011	56,894,440	725,152	−7,882,547	1,490,044	−1,003,984
C.R. Alessandria	319,244,620	6,317,761	271,568,276	1,659,906	9,078,250	−29,582,312	9,324,959	−1,205,797
C.R. Carpi	316,778,882	4,248,402	276,555,489	2,805,939	5,119,352	−459,986	6,716,784	−424,470
C.R. Pistoia e Pescia	297,538,636	6,686,002	207,652,727	146,969,052	5,687,109	−252,450	8,032,561	−425,984
C.R. Pesaro	272,040,007	9,879,435	213,835,353	58,490,282	2,222,048	−6,872	9,250,724	−296,546
Banco di Sicilia	267,946,422	2,773,352	254,304,536	15,088,711	1,933,637	0	1,218,290	−981,463
C.R. Macerata	264,524,477	10,159,438	197,833,071	72,451,410	2,282,203	−1,134,092	7,842,495	−414,037
M. Bologna e Ravenna	221,485,873	17,087,794	209,321,695	26,260,318	3,350,046	−917,544	17,183,342	−638,751
C.R. Biella	216,667,388	5,531,804	154,530,586	78,150,869	1,706,713	−63,346	7,965,586	−313,570
C.R. Pescara e LA	209,001,596	586,951	33,878,330	171,491,397	8,792,030	−650,000	7,283,761	−321,798
Total	**5,963,149,959**	**130,443,834**	**4,794,024,452**	**1,337,634,850**	**84,465,967**	**−69,841,027**	**158,800,074**	**−10,188,922**

Table A.8 Relevant financial statement items – medium bank foundations (2011)

Foundation name	Net assets (€)	Dividends and similar income (€)	Financial investments (€)	Current financial assets (€)	Interests and similar income (€)	Net revaluation of financial assets (€)	Operating surplus (€)	Boards' payments (€)
C.R. Livorno	206,030,319	3,053,413	154,348,935	21,353,652	3,690,729	−4,045,730	7,754,356	−242,501
C.R. Tortona	205,885,064	223,591	105,527,351	87,853,277	2,911,935	−630,548	1,169,934	−184,245
C.R. Asti	203,162,427	8,544,558	194,042,969	3,000,000	1,102,445	0	7,571,195	−635,632
C.R. La Spezia	200,916,376	3,969,030	118,624,363	93,043,889	579,364	−1,624,759	4,399,539	−596,160
C.R. Ferrara	181,880,327	200,000	200,850,302	0	68,911	0	−890,375	−482,969
C.R. Savona	176,107,898	5,295,546	176,374,412	0	2,969,288	−1,723,842	5,718,112	−343,451
C.R. Reggio Emilia	175,561,724	7,053,236	167,581,649	26,992,320	749,410	−9,321,403	−3,005,196	−337,139
C.R. San Miniato	174,679,170	1,184,287	171,890,169	0	1,066,979	0	1,185,262	−376,734
C.R. Gorizia	168,538,826	4,581,927	123,206,767	49,475,363	536,442	−518,319	3,707,811	−324,631
C.R. Ascoli Piceno	166,761,567	1,962,996	69,883,761	93,662,432	10,289	0	1,091,925	−340,200
C.R. Teramo	161,435,373	6,512,277	138,803,490	33,502,260	1,718,269	−498,187	6,804,658	−559,770
C.R. Imola	160,969,826	2,962,013	103,869,118	130,773,810	3,318,920	−6,651,191	4,892,919	−506,518
C.R. Fano	159,210,492	1,979,854	130,201,696	5,821,011	2,912,046	−413,315	4,701,419	−245,558
C.R. Carrara	154,305,241	2,128,758	111,174,332	38,709,012	992,604	−1,788,715	614,014	−350,179
C.R. Terni e Narni	154,285,806	3,270,178	143,626,238	18,559,197	3,989,399	−1,256,041	5,454,525	−200,278
C.R. Ravenna	153,611,655	12,005,611	129,707,314	24,657,929	864,758	−1,295,629	9,967,410	−454,506
C.R. Volterra	149,714,185	544	104,079,891	44,648,616	1,694,692	0	1,110,927	−303,453
C.R. Rimini	137,281,404	200,000	118,797,162	24,111,596	947,222	−1,201,501	2,073,115	−405,017
Total	**3,090,337,680**	**65,127,819**	**2,462,589,919**	**696,164,364**	**30,123,702**	**−30,969,180**	**64,321,550**	**−6,888,941**

Table A.9 Relevant financial statement items – medium-small bank foundations (2011)

Foundation name	Net assets (€)	Dividends and similar income (€)	Financial investments (€)	Current financial assets (€)	Interests and similar income (€)	Net revaluation of financial assets (€)	Operating surplus (€)	Boards' payments (€)
C.R. L'Aquila	136,502,223	1,266,362	93,152,376	40,122,291	2,597,828	635,097	1,166,607	−335,127
M. Parma	124,963,744	0	15,118,143	3,106,150	922,192	179,137	3,343,794	−322,443
C.R. Mirandola	121,330,652	307,789	26,937,247	97,301,036	2,683,844	−23,681	3,403,979	−111,399
C.R. Cesena	120,202,661	2,195,698	121,902,356	160,000	39,491	0	2,375,501	−259,457
C.R. Puglia	118,563,266	0	119,914,022	10,950	5,549,788	0	4,381,529	−392,129
Banco di Napoli	117,449,251	1,418,284	107,460,847	0	5,550,888	−389,808	625,216	−659,004
C.R. Vercelli	111,266,309	1,180,755	81,808,365	33,524,778	2,259,336	−32,100	1,520,780	−232,621
C.R. Jesi	102,977,731	4,517,981	68,504,843	1,063,049	792,373	0	3,941,180	−446,847
C.R. Rieti	100,430,174	1,561,581	80,832,719	13,630,958	1,309,364	0	1,780,503	−527,787
C.R. Prato	91,415,801	173,783	67,864,600	23,327,946	1,478,595	0	7,054,949	−158,728
C.R. Fermo	91,393,162	1,234,780	80,280,360	14,802,242	487,503	0	1,048,505	−258,403
C.R. Chieti	89,087,871	600,000	77,168,471	2,300,374	102,108	0	436,308	−351,403
C.R. Vignola	79,174,874	275,932	5,140,244	75,120,639	1,415,497	0	1,749,658	−220,305
C.R. Fabriano e C.	75,933,710	485,634	66,201,104	20,688,668	1,740,429	−277,577	834,387	−176,928
C.R. Calabria e Lucania	75,536,163	300,000	46,789,382	28,609,888	1,356,017	25,748	462,461	−281,389
C.R. Foligno	74,219,738	637,554	9,802,318	59,199,647	1,189,220	328,774	1,380,187	−290,601
B.M. Lucca	74,966,223	2,192,869	46,650,611	30,156,418	841,589	0	1,874,727	−269,175
Total	**1,705,413,553**	**18,349,002**	**1,115,528,008**	**443,125,034**	**30,316,062**	**445,590**	**37,380,271**	**−5,293,746**

Table A.10 Relevant financial statement items – small bank foundations (2011)

Foundation name	Net assets (€)	Dividends and similar income (€)	Financial investments (€)	Current financial assets (€)	Interests and similar income (€)	Net revaluation of financial assets (€)	Operating surplus (€)	Boards' payments (€)
C.R. Orvieto	66,869,155	1,677,067	23,403,391	42,072,719	587,362	0	1,931,893	−164,618
C.R. Spoleto	55,712,002	1,164,513	40,451,576	12,124,971	790,206	7,019	1,211,399	−219,207
C.R. Cento	55,238,261	935,479	44,423,538	15,626,547	262,452	−12,753	549,000	−222,364
B.N. delle Comunicazioni	54,826,451	2,050,567	12,045,277	74,764,502	1,344,228	−17,027,158	−32,920,375	−282,553
C.R. Fossano	51,060,698	2,758,569	47,384,239	7,548,463	176,893	−463,057	2,118,090	−263,053
C.R. Civitavecchia	50,641,392	2,461,272	44,629,480	0	686,394	0	1,974,841	−391,866
C.R. Saluzzo	42,013,032	1,700,363	35,968,239	8,784,228	229,465	−459,444	1,040,410	−168,407
C.R. Salernitana	39,431,408	1,245	854,607	36,773,104	399,915	−309,518	−99,556	−83,085
C.R. e B.M. Lugo	35,617,995	833,659	25,418,372	0	185,561	0	1,049,298	−232,558
C.R. Savigliano	34,825,886	1,041,726	30,462,167	6,249,925	125,354	130,078	855,826	−67,656
C.R. Viterbo	34,568,455	1,332,498	12,989,693	26,059,246	31,917	−118,193	−683,401	−200,327
B.M. Foggia	32,226,036	410,611	31,842,621	0	1,137,465	0	1,100,790	−102,337
C.R. Loreto	29,590,588	1,044,163	9,926,368	19,129,237	11,809	−120,628	302,987	−119,571
C.R. Città di Castello	27,837,781	169,152	9,307,942	13,877,873	320,462	0	337,110	−34,701
C.R. Bra	25,896,533	618,727	23,626,800	2,946,171	96,720	0	483,663	−130,003
B.M. e C.R. Faenza	17,276,762	349,734	17,582,876	0	3,055	0	374,891	−49,535
B.M. Rovigo	6,890,324	28,570	6,878,244	108,158	199,888	0	111,284	−63,136
Monte di Pietà di Vicenza	1,713,710	124,335	1,353,641	0	3,807	0	98,511	−16,636
Total	**662,236,469**	**18,702,250**	**418,549,071**	**266,065,144**	**6,592,953**	**−18,373,654**	**−20,163,339**	**−2,811,613**

A.3 Local Stakeholder Groups

Following, we present the total codex collected for identify the six stakeholder categories. For methodological reasons, we list both the codex in English translation and the Italian original version.

Public Sector

- Prefect (*Prefetto*).
- President of regional council (*Presidente della Giunta Regionale*).
- Presidents of Istituto Banco di Napoli (*Presidenti Istituto Banco di Napoli*).
- Foundation of regional councils of Abruzzo, Basilicata, Calabria, Lazio, Molise and Puglia (*Fondazione delle Giunte Regionali di Abruzzo, Basilicata, Calabria, Lazio, Molise e Puglia*).
- President of provincial council of Naples (*Presidente della Giunta Provinciale di Napoli*).
- Major of the city (*Sindaco della Città*).
- Municipality (*comune*).
- Other neighboring municipalities (*altri comuni limitrofi*).
- Region (*regione*).
- President of the Province, chosen among people operating in volunteering (*Presidente della Provincia scelto fra personalità attive nel volontariato*).
- Provincial administration (*amministrazione provinciale*).
- Municipal administration (*amministrazione comunale*).
- Ministry of Economy and Finance (*Ministero dell'Economia e delle Finanze*).
- Provincial councils (Consigli provinciali).
- Regional councils (Consigli regionali).
- People involved in public administration (Espressione della pubblica amministrazione).
- Superintendence for the Environmental, Architectural, Artistic and Historic Heritage of Perugia (*Soprintendenza per i beni Ambientali, Architettonici, Artistici e Storici di Perugia*).
- President of the Comunità Montana Appennino Pistoiese (*Presidente della Comunità Montana Appennino Pistoiese*).
- Governing board of UPI Puglia (*Comitato Direttivo dell'UPI Puglia*).

Culture, Education, and Research

- Rectors of universities (*Rettori delle Università*).
- Academy of Sciences of Turin, after alternating consultation with the class of physical, mathematical and natural sciences and the class of moral, historical

and philological sciences (*Accademia delle Scienze di Torino, sentita alternativamente la classe di Scienze fisiche, matematiche e naturali e la classe di Scienze morali, storiche e filologiche*).

- Accademia Nazionale dei Lincei, after alternating consultation with the class of moral, historical and philological sciences and the physical, mathematical and natural sciences class (*accademia Nazionale dei Licei, sentita alternativamente la classe di Scienze morali, storiche e filologiche e la classe di Scienze fisiche, matematiche e naturali).*
- President of the European University Institute (*Presidente dell'Istituto Universitario Europeo*).
- University Institute of Advanced Studies (*Istituto Universitario di Studi Superiori*).
- President of the Accademia dei Georgofili, chosen among the scholars of natural environment and/or landscape (*Presidente dell'Accademia dei Georgofili, scelto fra gli studiosi dell'ambiente naturale e/o del paesaggio*).
- President of the dell'Accademia Toscana di Scienze e Lettere "La Colombaria" (*Presidente dell'Accademia Toscana di Scienze e Lettere "La Colombaria").*
- Presidents of the following institutes: Carlo Besta Neurological Institute, Maugeri Foundation, Mondino Foundation and the European Institute of Oncology (*Presidenti dei seguenti Istituti: Istituto Neurologico Carlo Besta, Fondazione Maugeri, Fondazione Mondino ed Istituto Europeo di Oncologia*).
- Directors of the civic museums of Pavia, Brescia and of the Pezzoli museum of Milan (*Direttori dei musei civici di Pavia, di Brescia e del Museo Poldi Pezzoli di Milano*).
- Academy of Sciences, Ferrarese Deputation of National History, Ferrariae Decus, Italia Nostra Section of Ferrara (*Accademia delle Scienze, Deputazione Ferrarese di Storia Patria, Ferrariae Decus, Italia Nostra Sezione di Ferrara*).
- Lucchese Academy of Sciences, Letters and Arts – Lucca, and the Giovanni Pascoli Foundation – Castelvecchio Pascoli (*Accademia Lucchese di Scienze, Lettere ed Arti – Lucca e dalla Fondazione Giovanni Pascoli – Castelvecchio Pascoli*).
- Festival Pucciniano Foundation – Torre del Lago, and Viareggio Carnival Foundation – Viareggio (*Fondazione Festival Pucciniano – Torre del Lago e dalla Fondazione Carnevale di Viareggio – Viareggio*).
- Council of school managers of Carpi, Novi di Modena and Soliera. (*Conferenza dei Dirigenti scolastici di Carpi, Novi di Modena e Soliera*).
- Academy of Fine Arts of Macerata (*Accademia di belle Arti di Macerata*).
- Association "Arena Sferisterio Teatro di tradizione" of Macerata (*Associazione "Arena Sferisterio Teatro di tradizione" di Macerata*).
- Mozzi-Borgetti Civil Library (*Biblioteca Comunale Mozzi Borgetti*).
- Olivieri Institute of Pesaro – library and museums (*Ente Olivieri Pesaro -biblioteca e musei*).
- Rossini Foundation of Pesaro (*Fondazione Rossini Pesaro*).
- State Conservatory "G.Rossini" (*Conservatorio Statale di Musica "G. Rossini"*).

- Agrarian Academy in Pesaro (*Accademia Agraria in Pesaro).*
- Raffaello Academy in Urbino (*Accademia Raffaello in Urbino*).
- Academy of fine arts of Urbino (*Accademia di Belle Arti di Urbino*).
- ISIA, Higher Institute for Artistic Industries of Urbino (*Istituto Superiore di Industrie Artistiche di Urbino*).
- Adriano Olivetti Institute for studies on Economy and Management of Ancona (*Istituto Adriano Olivetti di Studi per la Gestione dell'Economia e delle Aziende – Ancona*).
- Organisations working in the field of culture (*Organizzazioni che operano nel settore della cultura*).
- Consortium for university education of Pordenone (*Consorzio di Pordenone per la formazione universitaria*).
- University Hospital (*Policlinico universitario*).
- Deputation of National History – Udine (*Deputazione di storia patria – Udine*).
- Pordenone Cultural Initiatives Centre (*Centro iniziative culturali Pordenone*).
- Teatro comunale di Bologna foundation (*Fondazione Teatro Comunale di Bologna*).
- "Casa di Oriani" Foundation – library and museum (*Fondazione "Casa di Oriani" – biblioteca, museo*).
- Flaminia Foundation for the university (*Fondazione Flaminia per l'università*).
- Deputation of National History for the Romagna Provinces (*Deputazione di Storia Patria per le Province di Romagna*).
- National academy of agriculture (*Accademia Nazionale di Agricoltura*).
- Cultural and political association "il Multino" (*Associazione di Cultura e di Politica "il Mulino"*).
- Studies Foundation of Cento, with management experience in the context of education (*Fondazione Patrimonio degli Studi di Cento, con esperienza dirigenziale nell'ambito della istruzione nel territorio di tradizionale radicamento ed operatività della Cassa di Risparmio di Cento*).
- Filopatridi Academy, Maderna Conservatory of Cesena, Malatesta Library of Cesena, in conjunction with each other (*Accademia dei Filopatridi, Conservatorio Musicale Maderna di Cesena, Biblioteca Malatestiana di Cesena, congiuntamente fra loro*).
- Albizzini Foundation – Burri Collection (exhibitions) (*Fondazione Albizzini – Collezione Burri (mostre)*).
- Association for University Settlements in the Province of Cuneo (*Associazione per gli Insediamenti Universitari in Provincia di Cuneo*).
- Merloni foundation – economomy, research, culture (*Fondazione Merloni – economia ricerca cultura*).
- Ente Giostra della Quintana – palio (*Ente Autonomo Giostra della Quintana di Foligno – palio*).
- Casa di studio Foundation Federico Sacco, Italia Nostra Section of Fossano, Commission of Sacred Art of the Diocese of Fossano (*Casa di Studio Fondazione Federico Sacco, Italia Nostra Sezione di Fossano, Commissione di Arte Sacra della Diocesi di Fossano*).

- Headmasters of the middle and high schools with seat in Fossano (*Presidi delle Scuole Medie inferiori e superiori con sede a Fossano*).
- Cultural association "Giuseppe Scarabelli" in Imola (*Associazione Culturale "Giuseppe Scarabelli" di Imola*).
- Studies centre "L. Einaudi" of Imola (*Centro Studi "L. Einaudi" di Imola*).
- Academy of Abruzzo – Pescara (*Accademia d'Abruzzo – Pescara*).
- School, Culture and Art Association – Pescara (*Associazione Scuola, Cultura ed Arte – Pescara*).
- Foundation for the promotion of the professional culture and economic development – Pescara (*Fondazione per la promozione della cultura professionale e dello sviluppo economico – Pescara*).
- Institute for Popular Drama of San Miniato Foundation (*Fondazione Istituto del Dramma Popolare di San Miniato*).
- "La ricerca" association, with seat in Piacenza (*Associazione "La Ricerca", con sede in Piacenza*).
- Protezionisti altoatesini (*Federazione Protezionisti altoatesini*).
- Historical society Pro Iulia Dertona of Tortona (*Società Storica Pro Iulia Dertona di Tortona*).
- President pro tempore of the European Community Commission, after consultation with CERN, ESA and the European University Institute (*Presidente pro-tempore della Commissione della Comunità Europea, sentiti il CERN, la ESA e l'Istituto Universitario Europeo*).
- Organisation of high prestige that deals with national-level education, training and protection of social media users (*ente di elevato prestigio che si occupa a livello nazionale di educazione, formazione e tutela degli utenti dei mezzi di comunicazione sociale*).
- Rossini Opera Festival Foundation of Pesaro (*Fondazione Rossini Opera Festival Pesaro*).
- Scientific institutes for research, hospitalization and care pursuant to current regulations and with seat in Lombardy (*Istituti di Ricovero e Cura a Carattere Scientifico ai sensi della vigente normativa e aventi sede in Lombardia*).
- State Archives of Chieti (*Archivio di Stato di Chieti*).

Trade and Professional Associations

- Regional unions of Chambers of Commerce, Industry, Handicraft and Agriculture of each Region (*Unioni Regionali delle Camere di Commercio, Industria, Artigianato e Agricoltura di ciascuna delle Regioni*).
- Provincial Chamber of Commerce, Industry, Crafts and Agriculture (*Camera di Commercio, Industria, Artigianato e Agricoltura della Provincia*).
- Chamber of Commerce, Industry, Craft and Agriculture of the other Provinces (*Camera di Commercio, Industria, Artigianato e Agricoltura di altre Province*).
- President of the local Chamber of Commerce (*Presidente della C.C.I.A.A. della città*).

- Land-reclamation cooperative of the Province of Ferrara (*Consorzi di Bonifica della Provincia di Ferrara*).
- President of the Industrialists' Union of Ferrara (*Presidente dell'Unione degli Industriali di Ferrara*).
- Provincial President of the Italian Federation of Artisans and Craftsmen of Ferrara (Presidente provinciale di Ferrara della Confederazione Nazionale dell'Artigianato e della piccola impresa).
- President of the provincial Confartigianato of Ferrara (*Presidente della Confartigianato provinciale di Ferrara*).
- President of the provincial Traders Association of Ferrara (*Presidente della Associazione Commercianti provinciale di Ferrara*).
- President of the provincial Confesercenti of Ferrara (*Presidente della Confesercenti provinciale di Ferrara*).
- President of the provincial Farmers' Federation of Ferrara (*Presidente della Federazione Provinciale Coltivatori Diretti di Ferrara*).
- President of the provincial Farmers' Union of Ferrara (*Presidente dell'Unione Provinciale degli Agricoltori di Ferrara*).
- Provincial presidents of the Italian Agricultural Confederation and the Small and Medium-sized Enterprises Association of Ferrara (*Presidenti provinciali di Ferrara della Confederazione Italiana Agricoltori e della A.P.I. Associazione piccole/medie industrie*).
- Orders of Architects, Lawyers, Chartered Accountants, Surveyors, Engineers, Doctors and colleges of Accountants and Notaries of Ferrara (*Ordini degli Architetti, degli Avvocati, dei Dottori Commercialisti, dei Geometri, degli Ingegneri, dei Medici e dai collegi dei Ragionieri e dei Notai di Ferrara*).
- More nationally-representative trade unions of transporters identified among personnel serving or retired FS Group SpA (*Organizzazioni sindacali dei trasporti maggiormente rappresentative a livello nazionale individuati tra il personale in servizio o in pensione del Gruppo FS S.p.A.*).
- Ministry of Infrastructures and Transport (*Ministero delle Infrastrutture e dei Trasporti*).
- Professional Orders (*Ordini professionali)*.
- Association of Industrialists of the Province of Macerata, Macerata provincial Union of Farmers, Association of Trade, Tourism and Services in the province of Macerata and Confartigianato of the province of Macerata (*Associazione degli industriali della provincia di Macerata, Unione provinciale degli agricoltori di Macerata, Associazione del commercio, del turismo e dei servizi della provincia di Macerata e Confartigianato della provincia di Macerata*).
- Confcommercio, Association of Trade, Tourism and Services (*Confcommercio, Associazione del Commercio, del Turismo e dei Servizi*).
- Italian Federation of Commercial Outlets and Tourist Agencies (*Confederazione Italiana Esercenti Attività Commerciali e Ausiliarie del Turismo*).
- Confartigianato, Provincial Craftsworker Association (*Confartigianato, Associazione degli Artigiani della Provincia*).

- CNA, National Confederation of Handicraft (*Confederazione Nazionale Artigianato*).
- Provincial Farmers' Federation (*Federazione Provinciale Coltivatori Diretti*).
- Provincial Farmers' Union (*Unione Provinciale Agricoltori*).
- Notary Council of United Districts of Pesaro and Urbino (*Consiglio Notarile dei Distretti Riuniti di Pesaro e Urbino*).
- Order of dDoctors (*Ordine dei medici*).
- Order of Lawyers (*Ordine degli avvocati*).
- Professional Orders of Surgeons and Dentists and of Pharmacists of the Ascoli Piceno province (*Ordini professionali dei Medici Chirurghi ed Odontoiatri e dei Farmacisti della provincia di Ascoli Piceno*).
- Wirtschaftsring and USB Economic and entrepreneurial organizations (*Organizzazioni economico-imprenditoriali Wirtschaftsring e USEB*).
- Provincial League of Cooperatives and Mutual organizations of Ferrara (*Lega Provinciale delle Cooperative e Mutue di Ferrara*).
- President of Confcooperative, provincial union of Ferrara (*Presidente della Confcooperative unione provinciale di Ferrara*).
- Two persons designated by the "Agreement for the Development of the Province of Cuneo" Association, formed by the Craftsmen Association, the Industrial Union, the Provincial Union of Traders and Merchants, the Provincial Union of Farmers, and the Provincial Farmers' Federation of the province of Cuneo (*Due soggetti dall'Associazione tra le Categorie Economiche "Patto per lo Sviluppo della Provincia di Cuneo", formato dall'Associazione Artigiani della Provincia di Cuneo, dall'Unione Industriale della Provincia di Cuneo, dall'Unione Provinciale Commercianti ed Esercenti di Cuneo, dall'Unione Provinciale Agricoltori di Cuneo, dalla Federazione Provinciale Coltivatori Diretti di Cuneo*).
- Agreement for the development (*Patto per lo Sviluppo*).
- President of the Provincial League of Cooperatives and Mutual Organizations of Ferrara (*Presidente della Lega Provinciale delle Cooperative e Mutue di Ferrara*).
- President of the Ferrara provincial union of Confcooperative (*Presidente della Confcooperative unione provinciale di Ferrara*).
- Provincial general secretaries of C.G.I.L., C.I.S.L. e U.I.L. of Ferrara (*Segretari Generali Provinciali di C.G.I.L., C.I.S.L. e U.I.L. di Ferrara*).
- The most representative provincial unions of employees and retirees (*Organizzazioni Sindacali provinciali dei lavoratori dipendenti e pensionati più rappresentative*).

Civil Society

- People that operate in the voluntary sector (*soggetti che operino nel settore del volontariato*).
- Regional Council for Voluntary – Piemonte (*Consiglio Regionale del Volontariato – Piemonte*).

- National Commission for Equality and Equal Opportunities between Men and Women (*Commissione Nazionale per la Parità e le Pari Opportunità tra Uomo e Donna*).
- Organization specified by the Board of Trustees, having its seat in a State member of the European Union and performing an institutional activity in one or more of the relevant sectors, (*ente avente sede in uno degli Stati membri della Unione Europea svolgente attività istituzionale in uno o più dei settori rilevanti, da indicarsi da parte del Consiglio Generale*).
- Presidents of the Lombardo Park in Ticino Valley, North Milan Park and the Mincio Park (*Presidenti del Parco Lombardo della Valle del Ticino, del Parco Nord Milano e del Parco del Mincio*).
- President of the Management Committee of the regional special Fund for volunteering service centres (*Presidente del Comitato di Gestione del Fondo speciale regionale per i Centri di Servizio per il Volontariato*).
- President of the Centre for Voluntary in the Province of Pavia, which identifies a set of candidates living in the Province of Pavia (*Presidente del Centro di Servizi per il Volontariato della Provincia di Pavia che individua una terna di nominativi aventi l'incolato in Provincia di Pavia*).
- A management expert, with competences also in non-profit organizations, chosen among the candidates indicated by the Board of Directors of the Banca Popolare Commercio e Industria SpA (*un esperto in management, anche con riferimento a soggetti non profit, scelto nell'ambito di una terna indicata dal Consiglio di Amministrazione della Banca Popolare Commercio e Industria S.p. A*).
- Association Ce.IS "Giovani e Comunità" Group, –Arciconfraternita di Misericordia and the– P.A. Humanitas Committee of the Green Cross – Lucca (*Associazione Ce.I.S Gruppo "Giovani e Comunità" – Lucca, dalla Arciconfraternita di Misericordia – Lucca e dalla Croce Verde – P.A. Comitato Humanitas – Lucca*).
- Organisation of high international prestige operating in case of humanitarian crises in areas hit by natural disasters or war (*ente di elevato prestigio che interviene a livello internazionale in presenza di crisi umanitarie, operando in particolare nei territori colpiti da calamità naturali o da eventi bellici, con risposte di solidarietà immediate e concrete*).
- Organisation with high reputation, nationwide and world-wide operating in the field of social distress also connected to emigration (*ente di ampia notorietà, operante a livello nazionale ed internazionale in materia di disagio sociale anche connesso al fenomeno dell'emigrazione*).
- Local environmentalist (*soggetto appartenente all'ecologismo locale*).
- Subject belonging to voluntary organizations (*soggetto appartenente all'ambiente del volontariato*).
- Permanent Conference of Volunteering and Social Promotion in the municipalities of Carpi, Novi di Modena and Soliera (*Conferenza permanente del Volontariato e della Promozione sociale nei Comuni di Carpi, Novi di Modena e Soliera*).

- Regional healthcare unit – Macerata (Azienda sanitaria unica regionale – Macerata).
- Marche Voluntary Association (*Associazione Volontariato Marche*).
- A person involved in Archdiocese of Bologna's voluntary activities (*espressione del volontariato assistenziale del centese, dall'Arcidiocesi di Bologna*).
- Local healthcare unit (*azienda sanitaria locale*).
- Segapeli, Lascito Cassarotti, Monti Torrioli Foundations – assistance and charity (*Fondazioni Segapeli, Lascito Cassarotti, Monti Torrioli – assistenza e beneficienza*).
- A.V.O. of Civitavecchia, CARITAS of Civitavecchia and UNITALSI of Civitavecchia.
- Social Assistance Consortium of Cuneo (*Consorzio Socio Assistenziale del Cuneese*).
- Administration of the S. Croce and Carle Hospital of Cuneo (*amministrazione dell'Azienda Ospedaliera S. Croce e Carle di Cuneo*).
- Management Committee of the Special Fund for Voluntary (*Comitato di Gestione del Fondo Speciale per il Volontariato*).
- Provincial Committee of the C.O.N.I. (*Comitato Provinciale di Cuneo del C.O. N.I.*).
- A.V.I.S.
- Lugo District Committee of the USL of Ravenna (*comitato di Distretto di Lugo dell'Azienda U.S.L. di Ravenna*).
- Local tourist offices (*pro loco*).
- A person within a triad proposed by the presidents of the regional sections of national environmental protection organizations operating in Lombardia (*un soggetto all'interno di una terna proposta dai Presidenti delle sezioni regionali lombarde delle Associazioni di protezione ambientale riconosciute di interesse nazionale dal Ministero dell'Ambiente ai sensi della vigente normativa e operanti in Lombardia*).
- A person chosen among four candidates proposed by the legal representative of the LILT (Lega Italiana Lotta ai Tumori – Puglia, of the IRCCS "Casa solievo della Sofferanza" – S. Giovanni Rotondo, of the IRCCS "Saverio De Bellis" – Castellana Grotte, of the AIRC (Associazione Italiana per la Ricerca sul Cancro) – Puglia. (*un soggetto fra quattro nominativi proposti dal Legale rappresentante della LILT (Lega Italiana lotta ai Tumori) – sez Puglia; Legale Rappresentante dell'IRCCS "Casa Sollievo della Sofferenza" di S. Giovanni Rotondo; Legale Rappresentante dell'IRCCS "Saverio De Bellis" di Castellana Grotte; Legale Rappresentante dell'AIRC (Associazione Italiana per la Ricerca sul Cancro) della Puglia*).
- Francesca, Valentina e Luigi Antonini Foundation – Spoleto (*Fondazione Francesca, Valentina e Luigi Antonini – Spoleto*).
- Olympic Academy of Vicenza (*Accademia Olimpica di Vicenza*).
- Ordinary diocesan of Florence, chosen among experts of sacred art (*ordinario Diocesano di Firenze, scelto fra gli esperti di arte sacra*).

- Person involved in Archbishop's curia, with expertise in the voluntary sector (*curia arcivescovile con competenze nel volontariato*).
- Bishop (*vescovo*).
- Diocese (*diocese*).
- Pio Sodalizio dei Piceni n Rome (*Pio Sodalizio dei Piceni di Roma*).
- Father Guardian of the Observance Convent of Bologna (*membro di diritto nella persona del Padre Guardiano, pro-tempore, del Convento dell'Osservanza di Bologna*).
- Confraternity of Mercy of Bra, founding institution of the pawnshop (*arciconfraternita della Misericordia di Bra, Ente fondatore del Monte di Pietà*).
- Nobile Arciconfraternita del Sacro Monte dei Morti of Chieti (*nobile Arciconfraternita del Sacro Monte dei Morti di Chieti*).
- Diocesan commission on sacred art and culture (*commissione diocesana di arte sacra e cultura*).
- Episcopal Conference of Puglia (*conferenza Episcopale Pugliese*).
- Pastoral Unit (*unità pastorale*).
- A member with recognized competence and experience in the field of environmental protection, chosen within a triad proposed by an association recognized by the Ministry of Environment which will be identified by the Board of Trustees (*un membro che abbia riconosciuta competenza ed esperienza nel settore della tutela dell'ambiente all'interno di una terna proposta da un'associazione di protezione ambientale riconosciuta dal Ministero dell'Ambiente che verrà individuata dal comitato d'indirizzo*).
- A member appointed jointly by the Port Authority of Livorno and the Port Authority of Piombino with reference to the goals of economic development in the maritime sector pursued by the foundation (*un membro designato congiuntamente dall'Autorità Portuale di Livorno e dall'Autorità Portuale di Piombino con riferimento agli scopi di sviluppo economico nel settore marittimo-portuale perseguiti dalla Fondazione*).

Board of Trustees

- Members appointed by the General Council among people of clear and undisputed reputation, who are able to integrate the skills already present in the Council (*membri nominati dallo stesso Consiglio Generale tra personalità di chiara e indiscussa fama in grado di integrare le competenze già presenti nel Consiglio*).
- Members co-opted by the Board itself (*cooptati da parte dello stesso Consiglio*).
- Six councillors chosen among people with specific professional qualifications and with expertise in foundation's institutional activities or in the management of economic and financial resources. Two members are appointed by the outgoing Board and four members are appointed by the succeeded Board of Trustees (*sei consiglieri scelti tra persone in possesso di specifici requisiti di professionalità e competenza nelle attività istituzionali della Fondazione ovvero*

nella gestione di risorse economico-finanziarie, così nominati: n.2 dal Consiglio di Indirizzo uscente; n.4 dal Consiglio di Indirizzo subentrato).

- Persons proposed by the President and co-opted by the Board of Trustees, chosen among people of high and undisputed reputation, expression of interest related to policy from time to time identified by the board of trustees (*su proposta del Presidente, mediante cooptazione da parte del Comitato di indirizzo, scelti fra personalità di chiara ed indiscussa fama, espressione degli interessi connessi ai settori di intervento di volta in volta individuati dal Comitato di indirizzo*).
- Members of high and undisputed reputation, co-opted by the Board of Trustees after a selective and comparative evaluation of the candidates proposed by qualified people or organizations operating within the Foundation's areas of intervention (*componenti di chiara ed indiscussa fama, nominati dal Consiglio di indirizzo per cooptazione, previa valutazione con criteri di tipo selettivo-comparativo, sulla base di candidature presentate da enti e aggregazioni della società civile operanti nei settori di attività della Fondazione e/o da personalità qualificate nei medesimi settori, secondo procedure precedentemente rese note attraverso pubblicazione sul quotidiano più diffuso nella regione*).
- Members of high and undisputed reputation, co-opted by the Board of Trustees (*componenti di chiara ed indiscussa fama, nominati dal Consiglio di indirizzo per cooptazione*).

Other

- Public or private national associations operating within the foundation's sectors of intervention (*enti o associazioni nazionali private operanti sull'intero territorio nazionale, nei settori d'interesse*).
- People who have distinguished themselves in scientific and cultural fields or who have gained particular expertise in promoting the socio-economic development of the territory (*persone che si siano distinte sul piano scientifico, culturale nei settori di intervento della Fondazione o che abbiano maturato particolari esperienze nella promozione di attività a vantaggio dello sviluppo socio economico del territorio*).
- People with professionalism, competence and experience –who can effectively contribute to the achievement of institutional goals (*personalità che, con l'apporto della propria professionalità, competenza ed esperienza – in particolare nei settori cui è rivolta l'attività della Fondazione – possono efficacemente contribuire al perseguimento dei fini istituzionali*).
- Public and private organizations representing the local community (*enti pubblici e privati espressivi delle realtà locali*).
- A member among people of high and undisputed reputation in the fields of social and health services (*un membro tra personalità di chiara ed indiscussa fama nei settori socio-sanitari e della salute*).
- A member who can contribute to the achievement of institutional goals (*un membro che possa contribuire al perseguimento dei fini istituzionali*).

- Five experts in the areas of intervention of the Foundation, including at least one member of the voluntary sector and one member of the culture and education sector *(cinque esperti nei settori di intervento della Fondazione di cui almeno uno esponente attivo del settore del volontariato e uno esponente del settore della cultura e della formazione, come da esito della pubblicazione di apposito bando secondo le procedure e le modalità stabilite dal regolamento)*.

A.4 Local Stakeholders Called to Define Members of the Board of Trustees

Table A.11 Local stakeholders called to define members of the Board of Trustees – foundations with assembly

Foundation name	Members of the Board Trustees (N)	Assembly of the original associates (%)	Public sector (%)	Culture, education, and research (%)	Trade and professional associations (%)	Civil society (%)	Board of Trustees (%)	Other (%)
Roma	20	50.00	0.00	25.00	0.00	5.00	20.00	0.00
Ente C.R. Firenze	22	50.00	22.73	18.18	4.55	4.55	0.00	0.00
C.R. Lucca	16	43.75	25.00	6.25	6.25	6.25	12.50	0.00
C.R. Bologna	28	50.00	21.43	7.14	10.71	10.71	0.00	0.00
C.R. Bolzano	28	50.00	25.00	7.14	7.14	10.71	0.00	0.00
C.R. Perugia	20	50.00	25.00	5.00	15.00	5.00	0.00	0.00
C.R. Pisa	24	50.00	20.83	12.50	12.50	4.17	0.00	0.00
C.R. Forlì	22	50.00	22.73	9.09	9.09	9.09	0.00	0.00
C.R Pistoia e Pescia	24	50.00	25.00	4.17	8.33	12.50	0.00	0.00
C.R Pesaro	30	50.00	23.33	6.67	6.67	13.33	0.00	0.00
C.R Macerata	26	50.00	15.38	3.85	19.23	11.54	0.00	0.00
C.R. Tortona	16	50.00	18.75	6.25	12.50	12.50	0.00	0.00
C.R. Livorno	24	50.00	25.00	4.17	12.50	8.33	0.00	0.00
C.R. Ferrara	52	48.08	11.54	5.77	28.85	1.92	3.85	0.00
C.R. San Miniato	25	48.00	24.00	4.00	8.00	12.00	4.00	0.00
C.R. Ascoli Piceno	20	45.00	20.00	5.00	10.00	10.00	10.00	0.00
C.R. Imola	20	50.00	15.00	15.00	10.00	10.00	0.00	0.00
C.R. Terni e Narni	20	50.00	25.00	0.00	20.00	5.00	0.00	0.00
C.R. Ravenna	16	50.00	12.50	6.25	12.50	12.50	6.25	0.00
C.R. Volterra	18	50.00	22.22	11.11	0.00	16.67	0.00	0.00
C.R. Rimini	18	50.00	16.67	0.00	27.78	5.56	0.00	0.00
C.R. L'Aquila	18	50.00	33.33	5.56	5.56	5.56	0.00	0.00
C.R. Cesena	20	50.00	20.00	10.00	10.00	10.00	0.00	0.00
C.R. Vercelli	14	50.00	21.43	0.00	7.14	7.14	14.29	0.00

C.R. Jesi	24	50.00	20.83	8.33	8.33	12.50	0.00	0.00
C.R. Rieti	20	50.00	35.00	0.00	5.00	10.00	0.00	0.00
C.R. Prato	14	50.00	14.29	14.29	21.43	0.00	0.00	0.00
C.R. Fermo	15	46.67	20.00	6.67	6.67	13.33	6.67	0.00
C.R. Chieti	16	50.00	25.00	12.50	6.25	6.25	0.00	0.00
C.R. Fabriano e C.	18	50.00	33.33	11.11	0.00	5.56	0.00	0.00
C.R. Foligno	20	50.00	25.00	10.00	10.00	5.00	0.00	0.00
C.R. Orvieto	10	50.00	20.00	10.00	10.00	10.00	0.00	0.00
C.R. Spoleto	22	50.00	22.73	9.09	4.55	4.55	0.00	9.09
C.R. Cento	23	47.83	17.39	8.70	17.39	4.35	4.35	0.00
C.R. Civitavecchia	14	50.00	21.43	7.14	14.29	7.14	0.00	0.00
C.R. Saluzzo	22	45.45	22.73	4.55	9.09	9.09	9.09	0.00
C.R. e B.M. Lugo	18	50.00	22.22	0.00	11.11	16.67	0.00	0.00
C.R. Viterbo	14	50.00	28.57	21.43	0.00	0.00	0.00	0.00
C.R. Loreto	12	50.00	16.67	0.00	0.00	33.33	0.00	0.00
C.R. Città di Castello	18	50.00	11.11	11.11	5.56	22.22	0.00	0.00
Monte di Pietà di Vicenza	8	0.00	50.00	12.50	12.50	25.00	0.00	0.00

Table A.12 Local stakeholders called to define members of the Board of Trustees – foundations without assembly

Foundation name	Members of the Board Trustees (N)	Public sector (%)	Culture, education, and research (%)	Trade and professional associations (%)	Civil society (%)	Board of Trustees (%)	Other (%)
C.R. Province Lombarde	40	22.50	5.00	0.00	10.00	35.00	27.50
San Paolo di Torino	21	28.57	14.29	28.57	9.52	0.00	19.05
Monte dei Paschi di Siena	16	87.50	6.25	0.00	6.25	0.00	0.00
C.R. Verona VI BL AN	33	42.42	15.15	6.06	15.15	3.03	18.18
C.R. Torino	24	50.00	4.17	8.33	4.17	33.33	0.00
C.R. Padova e Rovigo	28	32.14	17.86	25.00	7.14	17.86	0.00
C.R. Cuneo	23	52.17	4.35	21.74	21.74	0.00	0.00
C.R. Parma e Busseto	12	33.33	8.33	16.67	16.67	25.00	0.00
C.R. Genova e Imperia	28	50.00	0.00	17.86	7.14	25.00	0.00
Cassamarca	9	33.33	22.22	11.11	0.00	33.33	0.00
Banco di Sardegna	18	50.00	22.22	0.00	11.11	16.67	0.00
C.R. Modena	20	45.00	15.00	10.00	15.00	15.00	0.00
B.M Lombardia	27	25.93	11.11	22.22	29.63	0.00	11.11
C.R. Di Trieste	16	31.25	6.25	18.75	0.00	0.00	43.75
Banco di Sicilia	23	8.70	0.00	0.00	0.00	0.00	91.30
Venezia	14	35.71	14.29	7.14	0.00	42.86	0.00
C.R Udine e Pordenone	24	29.17	25.00	29.17	0.00	0.00	16.67
Piacenza e Vigevano	25	36.00	16.00	12.00	24.00	12.00	0.00
C.R Trento e Rovereto	18	44.44	27.78	27.78	0.00	0.00	0.00
C.R Alessandria	14	50.00	0.00	0.00	7.14	42.86	0.00
C.R Carpi	19	31.58	10.53	21.05	21.05	15.79	0.00
M. Bologna e Ravenna	24	37.50	41.67	16.67	4.17	0.00	0.00
C.R. Biella	15	26.67	6.67	13.33	13.33	40.00	0.00
C.R. Pescara e LA	9	33.33	33.33	0.00	0.00	33.33	0.00
C.R. Asti	21	47.62	0.00	23.81	0.00	28.57	0.00
C.R. La Spezia	18	33.33	0.00	22.22	5.56	11.11	27.78
C.R. Reggio Emilia	13	30.77	7.69	30.77	15.38	15.38	0.00
C.R. Savona	14	42.86	0.00	21.43	7.14	28.57	0.00
C.R. Gorizia	17	41.18	11.76	17.65	11.76	17.65	0.00
C.R. Teramo	10	50.00	10.00	10.00	0.00	30.00	0.00

(continued)

Table A.12 (continued)

Foundation name	Members of the Board Trustees (N)	Public sector (%)	Culture, education, and research (%)	Trade and professional associations (%)	Civil society (%)	Board of Trustees (%)	Other (%)
C.R. Carrara	14	50.00	14.29	21.43	7.14	0.00	7.14
C.R. Mirandola	15	46.67	13.33	13.33	26.67	0.00	0.00
M. Parma	10	40.00	10.00	20.00	10.00	20.00	0.00
Banco di Napoli	28	39.29	21.43	25.00	10.71	0.00	3.57
C.R. Puglia	12	0.00	25.00	25.00	16.67	33.33	0.00
B.N. delle Comunicazioni	15	33.33	6.67	40.00	20.00	0.00	0.00
C.R. Vignola	15	40.00	20.00	13.33	0.00	26.67	0.00
C.R. Calabria e Lucania	24	41.67	0.00	16.67	8.33	33.33	0.00
B.M. Lucca	12	50.00	16.67	25.00	8.33	0.00	0.00
C.R. Fossano	17	41.18	11.76	11.76	11.76	0.00	23.53
C.R. Salernitana	10	40.00	10.00	40.00	0.00	10.00	0.00
C.R. Savigliano	12	50.00	8.33	16.67	16.67	8.33	0.00
B.M. Foggia	11	36.36	9.09	9.09	45.45	0.00	0.00
C.R. Bra	10	40.00	0.00	20.00	10.00	30.00	0.00
B.M. e C.R. Faenza	11	27.27	9.09	18.18	27.27	18.18	0.00
B.M. Rovigo	5	40.00	0.00	20.00	0.00	40.00	0.00

MIX
Papier aus verantwortungsvollen Quellen
Paper from responsible sources
FSC® C105338

If you have any concerns about our products,
you can contact us on
ProductSafety@springernature.com

In case Publisher is established outside the EU,
the EU authorized representative is:
Springer Nature Customer Service Center GmbH
Europaplatz 3, 69115 Heidelberg, Germany

Printed by Libri Plureos GmbH
in Hamburg, Germany